Medicare 2020: The Simple A-Z Medicare Guide In 2020

By: Jay Howell

Table of Contents

3

Introduction

Why on earth would anyone read a book talking about Medicare of his or her own free will?

So why would you go about the trouble of actually reading this or any other book having to do with Medicare?

Honestly, you will want to read this book because there is just far too much information and misinformation regarding Medicare. It is something that basically everyone will need at a certain point in their lives but which hardly anyone understands.

It is an ofttimes painful, confusing, and generally mind numbingly dull subject to most people. But failing to educate yourself properly regarding Medicare may generate a lot of problems for you in the near future.

Just a Little Titbit about How Medicare Came into Being and How It Affects Us Today

The Medicare program was developed and introduced in the United States in the 1960s to allow Americans who are more advanced in years to better manage the increasing and otherwise unmanageable costs associated with health care and health insurance.

Over fifty years later, we as Americans have become burdened with the top-heavy, massive, and cumbersome bureaucracy into which Medicare has unfortunately morphed. It now serves to confuse the people whom it is intended to help and acts as a vehicle for a host of unscrupulous types to take advantage of the existing widespread confusion regarding the Medicare system in order to turn a profit from said confusion.

So What Are the Problems? (The Two Common Misconceptions Regarding Medicare)

Because of all the aforementioned confusion, bureaucracy, and unscrupulous profiteers, those who are approaching the age at which they will need Medicare have oftentimes fallen victim to one of two common, enormous, and somewhat opposing misconceptions.

- Misconception 1: The first common misconception is that you have to learn every single detail of the Medicare program or else you will run the risk of making one or more critical errors, errors which will ultimately ruin your life and make you completely and utterly miserable and wretched.

- Misconception 2: The second common misconception (which is admittedly somewhat at cross purposes with the first misconception) is that Medicare is too impossibly complicated to understand, so as a result, you should not even bother to learn anything about it at all and you should simply place your complete faith in the knowledge and machinations of a Medicare "adviser," a Medicare "consultant," or a Medicare "expert," who is also most likely a licensed insurance agent or a licensed insurance broker.

A Deeper Dive into Those Misconceptions

Now why on earth would anyone actually desire to learn every tiny little detail regarding Medicare? Seriously? Why would anyone go to the trouble of expending so much valuable time

9

and effort attempting to educate himself or herself about all the ins and outs of such a mind numbing and painfully dull matter? The first misconception has no doubt gotten a lot of people approaching the age at which they will start needing to worry about Medicare and its issues needlessly stressed and anxious.

This is the point at which the aforementioned Medicare "adviser," Medicare "consultant," or Medicare "expert" comes into play. A person who deems himself or herself as such is almost always a licensed insurance agent or a licensed insurance broker. These are the people from whom you are generally supposed to purchase health insurance policies, usually due to the mandates set in place by the various states which govern the brokerage and sale of any health insurance product that may be related to Medicare.

The Medicare "advisers," Medicare "consultants," and Medicare "experts" have not only been licensed by the state in which they are allowed to sell insurance products. This select group of people have helped to create and to perpetuate a widespread belief that these people are the only one who are capable of guiding the many helpless and hopelessly lost souls who are more advanced in years through the dark and wild jungle that is the Medicare system, out of the night and the dark woods and into the light, the bright eternal sunlight of everlasting joy and happiness.

So why have these Medicare "advisers," Medicare "consultants," and Medicare "experts" put such a vast amount of effort into developing and perpetuating this belief that they are the ones whom you ought to trust beyond a shadow of a doubt in order to lead you safely through the otherwise impenetrable forest known as the Medicare system?

Here is the quick and easy answer: It is due to the baby boom that happened in the United States in the middle of the twentieth century.

You remember, don't you? After World War II was finally over, there was a dramatically huge increase in the number of babies which were being born. This phenomenon lasted for a period of nearly 20 years. The babies who were born during this time became known as the baby boomers, as you most likely already know. If you are reading this book, there is a good chance that you yourself are, in fact, a baby boomer. The official definition which has been set forth by the United States Census Bureau states that a baby boomer is a person who was born between the years of 1946 to 1964 (inclusive).

Thus, according to the definition set forth by the US Census Bureau, the oldest group of these baby boomers reached the age of 65 in the year 2011, and the youngest group of these baby boomers will attain the age of 65 in the year 2029. So we are currently right smack dab in the middle of this nearly 20 year period in which all the baby boomers are reaching 65 years of age.

The United States has a current population of approximately 330 million people. Guess how many of those are baby boomers? The number lies at around 73 million people. 73 million! Out of 330 million! That means that a little more than 22 percent (more than one fifth or nearly one fourth) of the entire United States population has reached the age of 65 within the last nine or so years or will reach the age of 65 within the next nine or so years. We are literally right in the middle of the largest generation so far ever to be the beneficiary of the Medicare system. The only generation that is larger in number than the baby boomer generation is the generation known as the Millennials, who are generally the children of the baby boomer generation. And even the millennials who were born the earliest will not be turning 65 for quite a while.

So to these Medicare "advisers," "consultants," and "experts," the baby boomer generation represents a literal gold mine, a fat, juicy turkey or steak just waiting to be carved up and eaten. Selling health insurance to the constituents of the baby boomer generation represents a big fat paycheck due to the insurance commissions that can be earned through a successful sale. Basically, the average person who brokers insurance makes quite a substantial portion of his or her income based on selling insurance to the people in the baby boomer generation.

So What Makes This Book Different?

So how exactly are the contents of this book about Medicare different from the information about coverage which you might be given by one of those licensed insurance agents or licensed insurance brokers? Why is the information given in this book better than the information given by one of those people?

Well, the following is a list of some of the critical differences you will find between the advice given in this book and the advice given by those insurance brokers or insurance agents (the Medicare "advisers," "consultants," and "experts"):

- The first difference is that the advice which will be given in this book will be significantly easier to comprehend than the advice which would be given by an insurance agent or insurance broker.

- The second difference is that the advice which will be given in this book might get you more of your money's worth when it comes to Medicare coverage. Basically, if you utilize the advice given in this book, the same amount of money (as you would have paid through an insurance agent or an insurance broker) will most likely go much farther and get you more and better coverage and protection. You may receive a bigger bang for your buck.

-   The third difference is that the advice which will be given in this book will enable you to go right up to your licensed insurance agent and to tell him or her exactly the product or products you want to buy and for what reason. You will not need the insurance agent or broker to guide you or cajole you or steer you or manipulate you into a decision of his or her choosing. You will be able to tell him or her precisely what you want from him or her without being on the receiving end of any of his or her persuasions, manipulations, or machinations.

So, the content of this book deals fairly handily with both of those common misconceptions in one fell swoop.

First of all, there is absolutely no need whatsoever to study and memorize all the ins and outs, the tiny little details, of Medicare. This is honestly a giant waste of your valuable time and effort. Don't even bother with trying to learn everything there is to know about Medicare. Why shouldn't you bother? Well, as was said earlier, it is a massively unwieldy and cumbersome system of bureaucracy. And knowledge, in this case, definitely does not mean power.

Knowing every single little fact or detail concerning Medicare will not enable you to make it better so that you will be able to get coverage or protection that is cheaper or that is better. And if you do happen to make an error or a few errors when it comes to your selection of Medicare coverage, it is by no

13

means the end of the world. Your life will not be miserable. Your mistakes regarding Medicare can, in fact, be corrected with a relative amount of ease. Most of the poor choices and the mistakes you might make concerning Medicare may be fixed in less than a year. Actually, the mistakes which may end up costing you the most money generally arise from a complete failure to act, such as the mistake of a late enrollment penalty.

Secondly, placing your faith completely, blindly, and wholly in the hands of those licensed insurance agents is also something that really should not be done. They are not the only ones who are able to guide you through the darkness of the woods without incident. In fact, their guidance is not always the best guidance you can receive, since it may understandably lean toward the side of advising you to purchase that which will grant them the highest commission.

The advice you will get from this book is free of any such incentive. I get no commission whatsoever if you follow the principles set forth in this book. I am simply trying to give you advice on how to get the best coverage and protection at the lowest price and to set that advice forth in a manner that is simple and easy to read, removing from you the impossible burden of having to learn everything there is to know about Medicare. Basically, I want to give you the simple yet cost effective and adequately protective version. The information that you actually need to know in order to get the cheapest and best coverage. That advice and that advice alone is what I offer to you in this book.

One Final Note

Here's the thing: you actually don't even need to read this whole book to get the advice you need to get the best Medicare coverage for the most reasonable price. A summary or restatement of everything you need to know in this book is contained in Chapter 13. Literally, if you flip (or scroll) to Chapter 13 of this book and ignore everything else, you can just follow the step by step guide in that chapter and get health insurance coverage that is just about as protective, good, and reasonably priced as is available.

So basically, for the average reader of this book, Chapter 13 is the brief, succinct version of what you need to know and do when it comes to enrollment in Medicare and obtaining sufficient health care coverage at a decent price.

Honestly. You pretty much need only Chapter 13. You may not need to read anything else. So if you want the shortest version of advice possible, go ahead. Skip ahead to Chapter 13 if you want. Tear out the pages. Bookmark the pages. Take a screenshot of the pages. Do whatever you need to do. I won't be offended if you skip ahead. After all, if you are an average reader, Chapter 13 will tell you everything you need to know and do. If you read only one bit of information about Medicare in your entire life, make it Chapter 13. And more likely than not, the steps listed in Chapter 13 will be all you will ever need to do.

Allow me to underscore this one final time:

Chapter 13 holds a succinct restatement of everything you as an average reader will need to know and to do when it comes to enrollment in the Medicare program. So go ahead; skip ahead if you like.

Terminology

What Is a Part, and What Is a Plan? What Is the Difference Between the Two?

Parts (Original)

Medicare was originally comprised of two components which were commonly known as *parts*. The two original components, Part A and Part B, covered and still cover the following:

Part A covers the treatment which you as a patient would receive in a skilled nursing care facility or a hospital (this is also known as inpatient treatment). Basically, Part A covers the treatment you receive when you are **admitted** as a patient to a hospital or a skilled nursing care facility from which you must later be discharged.

Part B covers the treatment which you as a patient would receive in a doctor's office, etc. (this is also known as outpatient treatment). Basically, Part B covers the medical treatment you receive without needing to be admitted to or discharged from a hospital or from a skilled nursing care facility. It can include things like a physical examination, a blood test, an X-ray, etc.

Parts (Added on later)

Later on, Medicare had some additional components added on to it piece by piece—two extra parts, Part C and Part D. These parts may be described as follows:

Part C is also commonly known as a Medicare "Advantage Plan" or as a Medicare Health Plan. Part C is a private insurance option which offers the coverage of Medicare Part A and Part B in one single plan. It may also include coverage for Part D, which we will get to in a moment. A Part C Advantage plan might also include coverage for extra services such as dental, vision, and hearing. However, at this time, please note that the Part C Medicare Advantage Plans are NOT RECOMMENDED.

Part D consists of Prescription Drug Plans (PDP) which serve to defray or cover the cost of the drugs or medication which may have been prescribed to you by your doctor.

Plans

The types of coverage which are intended to serve as a supplement to Medicare coverage are known as *plans*. These plans include Medicare supplement plans and prescription drug plans (PDPs).

Medicare Supplement Plans serve to protect you against any coverage gaps in Medicare Part A and Part B. Basically, a supplement plan is intended to help to cover whatever Original Medicare (Part A and Part B) fail to cover.

Prescription Drug Plans, as described above, are plans which help to cover the cost of your prescription medication.

What Will Be Covered by this Book?

This book includes a discussion of only the four following items: Medicare Part A and Part B, the Medicare Supplement Plans, as well as the Prescription Drug Plans (PDPs).

Together, these four items will provide you with the best coverage and protection available. That is why they are the main items which will be discussed in this book.

Chapter 1: Who might you be and what do you need from this book?

Who will not find this book helpful

Okay, first of all, let me get this out of the way. This book is obviously geared toward persons who are in need of or who will soon be in need of Medicare. That is, this book is for persons at or nearing the age of Medicare eligibility, which is 65 years of age. Not only that, but it is geared toward the *average* person who needs or will soon need Medicare.

Now what exactly do I mean by *average*? Well, for the purposes of this book, an *average* reader is one whose health is in an average condition or better, one who possesses financial resources of an average amount or better, and one who lacks any desire to waste one's valuable time and effort in studying and memorizing the minutia in regards to Medicare.

So, if the condition of your health is below average or downright poor (for example, if you are suffering from a debilitating illness), the advice contained in this book is not for you. Also, if your finances are below average or perhaps even close to nonexistent, the advice found in this book is also not for you.

If you are not an average reader and any or all of the above situations apply to you (that is, that you suffer from a debilitating disease and/or are financially destitute), then you ought to stop reading this book. Instead, seek help from the Medicaid (for those on welfare or those with low income) office of the state in which you reside, and contact a licensed insurance agent who lives and operates in your immediate vicinity. The majority of regions in the United States offer at least one "special needs plan" which is intended to help those who may be destitute or in exceedingly poor health and is available to you locally. Basically, these types of plans are designed to help you when you are desperate and at your potential lowest point.

Just to recap, if you are destitute and/or suffer from a debilitating illness, please stop reading this book immediately and return it (if possible) for a refund of your money. This book will be of no help to you at all.

So Who Are You, Then?

Are you still reading? Okay, then you must be an *average* reader who needs Medicare or who will soon be in need of Medicare.

So who might you be and what exactly do you want?

Are you about to reach the age of Medicare eligibility?

Are you perhaps reading this book so that you can offer advice to one of your relatives or one of your friends?

Are you thinking of leaving health insurance coverage which is connected to your job?

Are you trying to determine whether or not the Medicare decisions you made a while ago were actually valid and sound decisions?

Are you just currently bored out of your mind due to the social distancing and frequent, thorough hand washing necessary to curb the spread of a certain virus?

What exactly are you looking for from this book?

The Purpose of This Book

Simply put, this book will offer you simple, straightforward guidance through the forest that is the Medicare system.

This book lays out a clear path for you to learn about and acquire the layers of health insurance coverage which are necessary for adequate protection under the Medicare system. The layers that you need are precisely the following four items:

- Medicare Part A
- Medicare Part B
- Medicare Supplement Plans
- Prescription Drug Plans (PDPs)

That's it. These four layers are all that you will require for complete coverage and protection under Medicare. The coverages which are offered by each of these four layers will most likely serve you exceedingly well for the next few decades of your life. You will not even need to review your Medicare situation on an annual basis or renew any part of your coverage except possibly whichever Prescription Drug Plan (PDP) you have selected, and you have to review that only if you wish to continue to ensure that the costs for your medical prescriptions remain as low as they can possibly be.

So the purpose and the goal of this book is to simplify a complicated subject and to offer you an easy to understand and straightforward method to getting complete coverage at a reasonable price.

Chapter 2: So what is Medicare, anyway, and what does it do?

Why is Medicare so important? Why do I care?

So let us say that there exists a hypothetical couple by the name of Mr. and Mrs. Walker. Mr. and Mrs. Walker reached the age of 65 and decided to follow a Medicare coverage enrollment path that happens to be identical to the one which will be laid out for you in this book.

First, Mr. and Mrs. Walker chose to sign up for Medicare with the government through the use of its specially designed website.

Then, Mr. and Mrs. Walker discovered that Medicare coverage is not sufficient on its own and has a bunch of flaws as well as gaps in coverage, so they decided to buy insurance that would serve to secure them against the weaknesses in their Medicare coverage. This type of insurance which they purchased in order to serve as a supplement to their Medicare plan is commonly known as, interestingly enough, a Medicare Supplement Plan. It's amazing what people come up with nowadays in terms of naming.

All jokes aside, Mr. and Mrs. Walker happen to have an adorable young grandkid by the name of Freddie who has a particular talent for spreading germs everywhere (like most of the children at his age). One day, after young Freddie visits his loving grandma and grandpa and they cover him in the requisite kisses and hugs, Grandma and Grandpa Walker both come down with severe cases of the flu due to Freddie's germ spreading abilities. Although Mr. and Mrs. Walker are ordinarily in average to good health, their overcoming this particularly nasty strain of the flu necessitates a trip to the hospital emergency room, their being admitted for inpatient treatment and discharged from the hospital, as well as a number of other appointments with their family practitioner in order to follow up on how their recovery is going after they get discharged from the hospital.

Mr. and Mrs. Walker expect that a number of staggering medical bills will begin arriving shortly after they have recovered from their illness, but to their surprise, this does not take place. Due to the protection they receive under their Medicare coverage, the invoices they were expecting to receive from the doctors, from the hospital, from the laboratory, from their family physician, etc. were all instead directed to the United States federal government to be paid by them. This was set in motion as soon as Mr. and Mrs. Walker handed their identification cards to the hospital staff at the time when they began their treatment.

The federal government (functioning as Medicare) calculates and pays its share of the medical bills for Mr. and Mrs. Walker. After this, the federal government notifies the insurance company through which Mr. and Mrs. Walker had purchased a Medicare Supplement Plan for themselves. The employees at the insurance company check again to make sure that the federal government has made its calculations correctly. After checking the calculations, the insurance company issues enough checks to cover the remainder of the balances due to all those who had provided the medical care to Mr. and Mrs. Walker during their unfortunate bout with the flu.

Several months after Mr. and Mrs. Walker recover fully from their bout with the flu, the financial impact and consequences of the sickness for which they received treatment is fully resolved in the following manner:

Mrs. Walker, in choosing a Medicare Supplement Plan earlier on, had chosen to take the most conservative route possible by buying the most luxurious, most comprehensive Medicare Supplement Plan available to her. This had resulted in her having to pay a premium of approximately $150 on a monthly basis. A number of months after she has fully recovered from her unexpected illness, she discovers to her great delight that all of her medical bills have been paid in full, meaning that the combination of her Medicare and the luxurious, comprehensive Medicare Supplement Plan she selected offered her 100 percent coverage for her illness and absolutely all of the treatment related to it.

Mr. Walker, never having been one to play it safe, when selecting a Medicare Supplement Plan for himself, had decided upon a low cost yet high performance Medicare Supplement Plan for which he had to pay a premium of a mere $50 on a monthly basis. Due to the fact that the supplement plan he chose (which is by no means as luxurious or as comprehensive as the one chosen by Mrs. Walker) carries a high deductible, Mr. Walker is required to write a number of checks which total a few hundred bucks in order to share the cost of his medical bills with the insurance company from whom he purchased his Medicare Supplement Plan. However, the fact that he saves about a hundred dollars a month (which is about twelve hundred dollars a year) in lower monthly premium payments (when compared to the luxury plan which was chosen by his wife) does more than enough to make up for the fact that he now needs to write checks for a few hundred dollars to cover his deductible.

Neither Mr. Walker nor Mrs. Walker is saddled with crippling and unmanageable medical bills due to their unexpected bout with a severe illness. This is because they happened to follow the path which will soon be laid out for you step by step in this book regarding their Medicare coverage.

And as you can see, no matter which Medicare Supplement Plan Mr. and Mrs. Walker originally decided to purchase for themselves, whether it was the comprehensive, luxurious plan opted for by Mrs. Walker or the low cost, high deductible yet high performance plan selected by Mr. Walker, neither of them was put into dire financial straits. Both of the plans they selected offered great coverage for them and were fairly financially feasible and manageable.

So what have we learned from this hypothetical tale? Well, hopefully it has enabled us to realize that the Medicare system is simply a mechanism for paying bills for the Americans who are covered by it. Why then does there seem to be such a fantastic brouhaha surrounding it?

Well, the simple fact of the matter is that insurance companies and the agents who sell health insurance policies are trying their best to derive as large a payday as possible from the fact that the baby boomer generation is coming of Medicare age. Insurance companies bombard Americans who are approaching the age of 65 with endless propaganda and severe warnings that navigating the system of Medicare without licensed professional guidance is an exercise in futility and stupidity. The licensed insurance agents and licensed insurance brokers who deem themselves "advisers" and "experts" in the subject of Medicare are more than willing to generate further confusion in their customers, which ultimately leaves those customers more vulnerable and more responsive to the commission-based, biased guidance they have to offer.

Other more well-meaning Medicare "advisers" or Medicare "consultants" may mistakenly advise those approaching the age of Medicare eligibility that in order for them to act responsibly, they must spend countless hours of their valuable time and loads of their precious effort perusing junk mail, studying and memorizing thick, clunky textbooks related to Medicare, meeting with officials of the government, and going to boring seminars designed to educate them about the system of Medicare. All of this serves to perpetuate the common misconception that if you fail to learn every single little itty bitty detail about the Medicare system, you will make a critical error that will bring you into financial ruin and an utterly miserable rest of your life.

Guess what? None of the above is true.

If you do not learn every single tiny little detail there is to know about the Medicare system, you will not make a horrible, egregious error that will ruin the rest of your life. Yes, you might make an error or two, but it will likely be not so severe, and it will be easily corrected within a year at most. Your life is not over if you make a bad decision regarding your Medicare enrollment. So there is no need for you to read every single scrap of paper that is sent to you regarding the steps you will take for your Medicare enrollment or to pore over those ridiculously dull Medicare textbooks. Don't worry. Making a mistake in your Medicare enrollment decisions will not spell out the end of the world for you. This book will even teach you how to fix those mistakes, and most of the time, fixing them is fairly simple and relatively painless.

Also, the insurance industry is mainly focused on earning the highest commissions possible from your purchase of health insurance. The licensed insurance agents and brokers will tell you all about the Medicare Advantage plans which offer them the riches schedules for commissions. They will promote these Advantage plans as if their lives depend on it. They might also then tell you about the Medicare Supplement plans for which these agents are not as well compensated in terms of their commission schedules. But these agents will almost certainly never ever tell you about the plan I recommend the most highly, which just so happens to be Medicare's best kept secret.

Dear reader, you too can be as well covered and protected by the Medicare system as the hypothetical Mr. and Mrs. Walker were in the time of the treatment of their illnesses for as reasonable of a price as each of them ended up having to pay. All you have to do is to follow the steps and advice which are being conveniently laid out for you in this book.

The Big Secret

So what is this secret? The secret that your insurance agent or broker will never, ever tell you about? Here are the two magic words that you will have to tell to your insurance broker or insurance agent in as forceful a manner as is necessary: high deductible.

Yes, the plan I recommend most highly is a high deductible plan. That is the secret. We will discuss this in much greater detail later on in this book (in Chapter 7, to be specific, in case you suddenly got the urge to skip ahead and to take a quick sneak peek).

Chapter 3: Medicare Part A

Okay; here we go. Your desire in reading this book ought to be to reduce to a bare minimum the amount of time and the amount of effort you will be required to spend in order to establish the health coverage you need that is related to Medicare.

We begin our discussion of what you really need to know about the Medicare system, logically enough, with Medicare Part A. This, if you recall from the terminology section, was one of the parts of the original system of Medicare which existed before other parts were added on to it (Original Medicare consisted of just Medicare Part A and Medicare Part B).

The following chapter will tell you everything you ever need to know about Medicare Part A. Really. What is contained in this chapter is literally everything you ever need to know about Medicare Part A, which is one of the four essential layers of Medicare related coverage.

What is Medicare Part A and why do I need it?

Medicare Part A is the health insurance which is offered by the United States federal government to those Americans who have reached the age of 65 or older. Medicare Part A is designed to reimburse to those who are covered by it a portion of or, ideally, all of the costs which are incurred during the treatment of a patient in inpatient facilities such as a hospital, a rehabilitation facility, and a skilled nursing care facility.

In almost every case, an American who has worked in the United States for ten or more years (or who is married to a person who has worked in the United States for ten or more years) and who has paid taxes on that employment will get Medicare Part A offered to him or her free of charge, with no cost whatsoever.

Due to the fact that Medicare Part A is free of charge, basically everyone is supposed to have enrolled in Medicare Part A by the time they reach their 65th birthday.

The coverage effective date, or the date on which a person's Medicare Part A coverage takes effect (as is the case with all coverages which are related to Medicare) always falls on the first day of the month in question.

Almost all of the time, a person who is about to reach the age of 65 may choose to enroll in Medicare Part A up to 3 months before the start of his or her birthday month. If a person chooses to apply early in this fashion, the coverage he or she will receive under Medicare Part A will take effect on the very first day of his or her birthday month (and not on the first day of the month in which he or she enrolled, if he or she chose to enroll in Medicare Part A before his or her birthday month came around).

In addition to the three month period of early enrollment in Medicare Part A, a person also has available to them the possibility of enrolling in Medicare Part A for a few months after his or her birth month has passed. However, enrolling late in this manner might possibly mean that the person must be without coverage by his or her health insurance during this period of time.

Note 1: This an exception to one of the above rules. If a person's actual date of birth happens to fall on the first of any month, his or her coverage under Medicare Part A (and under any other coverage associated with or related to Medicare) will take effect on the very first day of the month prior to his or her birthday month. You can try to ask what the reason for this is, but honestly, it is pretty likely that no one has any idea why this might be the case.

Note 2: This is a second exception, this time relating to the timeline related to a person's enrollment in Medicare Part A. If a person has an existing health insurance policy that is a Health Savings Account (HSA) and he or she wishes to continue to offer pre-tax contributions, he or she may want to consult with an expert regarding the delaying of his or her enrollment in Medicare Part A, since the coverage offered by Medicare Part A might preclude deductible contributions to an HSA plan.

How do I enroll in Medicare Part A?

It is actually surprisingly easy to enroll in Medicare Part A. In fact, the entire process of enrollment in Medicare Part A using the following website may even take you as little as or perhaps even fewer than ten minutes in total.

The link directly below is where you can go online in order to enroll yourself in Medicare Part A; the website is quite user-friendly and for the most part self-explanatory:

https://www.ssa.gov/medicare/

Also, please do not be bothered at all if the above link happens to redirect you to the following link:

https://www.ssa.gov/benefits/medicare/

Both of these links link to exactly the same website (the one through which you can apply for Medicare Part A easily and as painlessly as possible).

Chapter 4: Medicare Part B

We now continue our discussion of what you really need to know about the Medicare system with, as continues to be logical, Medicare Part B. This, if you recall from the terminology section, was also one of the parts of the original system of Medicare which existed before other parts were added on to it (Original Medicare consisted of just Medicare Part A and Medicare Part B).

The following chapter will tell you everything you ever need to know about Medicare Part B. Seriously. The advice and information which is divulged in this chapter is actually everything you will ever need to know about Medicare Part B, which is the second item of the four essential layers of Medicare related coverage.

What is Medicare Part B and why do I need it?

Medicare Part B is the health insurance which is offered by the United States federal government to those Americans who have reached the age of 65 or older. Medicare Part B is usually designed to reimburse to those who are covered by it a portion of or, ideally, all of the costs which may be incurred during the treatment by a doctor or doctors of a patient in an outpatient capacity such as in a doctor's office, etc. as well as the expenses which may be incurred for testing and diagnostics, medical supplies, medical equipment, and preventative health care.

Recall that outpatient care relates to treatment which a patient receives without needing to be admitted to a hospital, a skilled nursing care facility, etc. Thus, Medicare Part B generally deals with the coverage for health care that is more on the routine side and is usually less severe.

The Timing Surrounding Your Enrollment in Medicare Part B

It is of vital importance that you know to select the effective date of the coverage which you receive under Medicare Part B with great care. This is the reason why: Medicare Part B comes at a substantial monthly cost. The monthly premium for Medicare Part B in the year 2020 starts at $144.60 per month. Because of this substantial cost, it would not be considered wise to start your coverage under Medicare Part B at too early of a time. If you decide to start Medicare Part B too early, you may end up paying a lot more than you ought to for your Medicare related health coverage.

On the other hand, due to the fact that Medicare Part B is a crucial layer of protection which is intended to reimburse you for the expenses incurred during those treatments which are most frequently encountered, it would be considered **exceedingly unwise** for you to start your coverage under Medicare Part B too late.

If one waits too long after he or she becomes eligible and chooses to enroll too late for Medicare Part B, he or she runs the risk of incurring hefty, staggering medical bills with zero protection from health insurance to help to defray the cost. Furthermore, if a person fails to enroll for Medicare Part B until the period of eligibility has passed entirely, then the opportunity for him or her to enroll in Medicare Part B will then be limited to just a brief period of time at the start of each of the following years, and the coverage received through this late enrollment in Medicare Part B will fail to take effect for a number of months after the late enrollment takes place.

In addition to that, any enrollment in Medicare Part B which may be considered substantially late will subject the person who enrolled late to a monetary penalty which will literally last a lifetime; this penalty is tacked onto the monthly premium forever (for as long as you have to pay the premium, which is equal to as long as you will live).

Thus, it is impossible to overstate the extreme important of enrolling in Medicare Part B in a timely fashion. Let me say this again. Enroll in Medicare Part B **ON TIME!** Otherwise, you may be subject to a long period of time without health coverage as well as a potential monetary monthly penalty which will last you the term of your natural life.

When to Enroll in Medicare Part B If You Are About to Reach the Age of 65

If you are solely responsible for your own health insurance coverage and you will soon be eligible for Medicare, then you ought to have absolutely no difficulty whatsoever when it comes to selecting the date on which you will enroll for Medicare Part B. When you are just about to reach the age of 65, you should enroll in Medicare Part B. After doing this, the effective start date of your coverage will be the very first day of the birth month in which you reach 65 years of age.

Your enrollment period for Medicare Part B will commence three months before the birth month in which you reach 65 years of age. Thus, you should aim to start the process of your enrollment in Medicare Part B as early within this period of 90 days as is practical for you and your finances (keeping in mind that enrolling early brings with it a substantial premium every month, but enrolling late will cause your premium each month to go even higher due to the added monthly penalty and will cause a host of other problems).

Note: This an exception to the above rule concerning the effective start date of a person's coverage. If a person's actual date of birth happens to fall on the first of any month, his or her coverage under Medicare Part B (and under any other coverage associated with or related to Medicare) will take effect on the very first day of the month prior to his or her birthday month. You can try to ask what the reason for this is, but honestly, it is pretty likely that no one has any idea why this might be the case.

When to Enroll in Medicare Part B If You Are Choosing to Retire from A Group Health Care Plan after Reaching the Age of 65

If you have already reached 65 years of age and you are planning to retire from a group medical plan, you ought to schedule your medical coverage to start on the date on which your group medical plan ends. It is rather unwise to allow for a gap in your insurance coverage, and to allow a gap which lasts longer than 63 days continuously is a bit of a disaster. After you have had a gap or a lapse in your medical coverage of more than 63 continuous days, your medical history might be called into question in order to determine when or if you will be permitted to possess full coverage for each and every medical condition.

Prior to your beginning the process of enrollment in Medicare Part B, you ought to download the following form off of the internet: Form CMS - L564. Then, you should have the Human Resources department of your employer complete the portion of the form which is relevant to them. Form CMS - L564 with the relevant portion filled out by your Human Resources department will serve to verify that your coverage in the medical plan offered by your company to you due to your status as an active employee lasted until the stated termination date.

With this form which proves the date of the termination of your group health care plan and with the fact that you should have scheduled the start of your coverage under Medicare Part B to coincide with the termination of your group plan, you will not be left with any gaps or lapses in your medical coverage.

What Other Circumstances or Situations Might Possibly Affect Your Decisions Regarding Coverage under Medicare Part B?

If any of the following conditions apply to you, then your decision regarding when to begin the enrollment process for Medicare Part B may be somewhat complicated:

- Do you not have United States citizenship?
- Are you married to a person who has active employment?
- Are you possibly eligible for any Veterans Affairs coverage such as Tricare?
- Are you enrolled in COBRA or medical coverage for retirees from a group plan offered by your employer?
- Do you perhaps belong to a different category which might complicate matters?

If the answer to any of the above questions for you is yes, then you might need to seek some advice from a professional regarding precisely when or whether you ought to begin your coverage under Medicare Part B.

The professional advice you seek out ought to be from one of the following unbiased and utterly solid resources which are listed and explained in some detail below.

How do I enroll in Medicare Part B?

Exceedingly similar to enrolling in Medicare Part A, it is actually surprisingly easy to enroll in Medicare Part B. In fact, the entire process of enrollment in Medicare Part B using the following website may even take you as little as or perhaps even fewer than ten minutes in total.

The link directly below is where you can go online in order to enroll yourself in Medicare Part B; the website is quite user-friendly and for the most part self-explanatory:

https://www.ssa.gov/medicare/

Also, please do not be bothered at all if the above link happens to redirect you to the following link:

https://www.ssa.gov/benefits/medicare/

Both of these links link to exactly the same website (the one through which you can apply for Medicare Part B easily and as painlessly as possible).

Other Solid Resources (besides this book)

Here are a number of wholly unbiased sources of advice and information which will inform you regarding the process of selecting the most suitable Medicare effective coverage date for you and/or your spouse.

Medicare.gov: For Finding Useful Contact Information Specific to a Particular State or Organization

The link to the website below allows you to obtain helpful contacts which will offer you advice and information that can be specific to the state in which you reside.

Medicare.gov is the official United States government site for Medicare, so you can be sure to receive unbiased, thorough information from this website. And this is the "Find contact information" page of that official government website.

The search function is quite simple and straightforward to use. First, simply select the state for which you need contact information and advice, and second, select the organization within that state the contact information of which you need. If you have no idea what the name of the organization you want is, you may simply select the "ALL organizations" option from the pull down menu. You can also narrow your search for your desired contact information even further if you choose to do so by selecting one or more topics of interest, such as "Complaints about my care or services," "Help with my Medicare options & issues," "Other insurance programs," "Claims & billing," "Health care facilities & services in my area," etc.

The webpage also includes some links to a number of other websites which may be helpful to you, as well as offering for download a "Helpful Contacts database."

https://www.medicare.gov/contacts/

The Social Security Administration (SSA): For Finding Information Derived Directly from the Governmental Body Which Is in Charge of the Medicare Program

The link to the website below provides you with comprehensive information regarding the benefits of Medicare.

The Social Security Administration (SSA) is the arm of the United States government which is responsible for administering and overseeing the entire Medicare program. This is the webpage of the Social Security Administration which is dedicated wholly to Medicare as well as its benefits.

Not only does this webpage contain substantive information about the benefits of Medicare, but it also just so happens to be the webpage you must use in order to apply online for both Medicare Part A and Medicare Part B. Not only that, but this webpage also contains a wide variety of links to information related to Medicare, including a number of relevant forms which may be downloaded from the website.

https://www.ssa.gov/medicare/

Also, please do not be bothered at all if the above link happens to redirect you to the following link:

https://www.ssa.gov/benefits/medicare/

Both of these links link to exactly the same website (the one through which you can apply for Medicare Part A and Medicare Part B easily and as painlessly as possible, and the one from which you can find information regarding the benefits of Medicare from the governmental organization which offers you those benefits).

Choosing a Medigap Policy: A Guide to Health Insurance for People with Medicare (2020)

The link to this PDF file below provides you with an official government guide from the Centers for Medicare and Medicaid Services (CMS), which is published by Medicare.gov.

Medicare.gov is the official United States government site for Medicare, so you can be sure to receive unbiased, thorough information from this website.

And this PDF document offered jointly by the Centers for Medicare and Medicaid Services (CMS) as well as the National Association of Insurance Commissioners (NAIC) through the Medicare.gov website is an official government guide which has important information about Medicare Supplement Insurance policies (also commonly known as Medigap policies or Medicare Supplement Plans), what is covered by these Medigap policies, the rights you possess in terms of buying a Medigap policy, and how you can buy a Medigap policy. Basically, this guide will be able to help you if you are thinking of buying a Medicare Supplement Insurance (Medigap) policy or if you already have such a policy. It will enable you to fully understand how such Medicare Supplement Insurance policies function.

https://www.medicare.gov/Pubs/pdf/02110-medicare-medigap-guide.pdf

Medicare and You 2020: The Official U.S. Government Medicare Handbook

The link to this PDF file below provides you with an official government guide from the Centers for Medicare and Medicaid Services (CMS), which is published by Medicare.gov.

Medicare.gov is the official United States government site for Medicare, so you can be sure to receive unbiased, thorough information from this website.

And this PDF document published by the Centers for Medicare and Medicaid Services (CMS), which is a government agency which operates within the United States Department of Health and Human Services (HHS), offered through the Medicare.gov website, is the official handbook regarding Medicare provided by the United States government. This official government handbook contains a thorough overview of the different parts and plans of Medicare, when and how to enroll in the parts of Medicare, and other such useful information regarding Medicare.

https://www.medicare.gov/Pubs/pdf/10050-medicare-and-you.pdf

The Human Resources Department of Your Company

This may seem like a strange or unlikely place to look for and find help related to Medicare, but when it comes to determining the right timing for the start date of your coverage under Medicare Plan B, the Human Resources department of your company probably has quite a bit of experience in filling out the appropriate form for you and letting you know of your exact group health plan coverage termination date.

Public Service Organizations or Agencies

There are certain public service organizations or agencies, such as your local county hospital, which may keep an advisor for Medicare and Social Security on staff. In such a case, this advisor most likely does not work for an insurance company and does not make a commission on anything he or she may advise you to buy. Thus, the advice from this hospital or public service agency Medicare and Social Security advisor is more likely to be completely without bias.

Medicare for Dummies Cheat Sheet

The link to the website below provides you with a cheat sheet for figuring out exactly what you need to know regarding the Medicare program.

Although this website is not an official Medicare website provided by the government, it still has plenty of virtues. We should not discount this website or resource simply due to its lack of "officialness." The "Dummies" brand has become famous for providing the general public with guides to just about every subject under the sun which are remarkably easy to read and easy to understand. This cheat sheet about Medicare has as its source one such guidebook regarding Medicare, entitled *Medicare for Dummies, 3rd Edition*.

The Medicare for Dummies Cheat Sheet itself contains a brief and succinct breakdown of three critical topics related to Medicare. The first topic is a helpful list of what to do and what not to do before you begin navigating through the Medicare program, the second topic is a speedy rundown of what the best periods of time to begin the enrollment process are, depending on the circumstances specific to your particular situation, and the third topic is a helpful mini directory of some organizations which you can contact in order to find help regarding any issues you may encounter with the Medicare program.

https://www.dummies.com/personal-finance/insurance/health-insurance/medicare-for-dummies-cheat-sheet/

State Health Insurance Assistance Programs (SHIP): For Finding Your Local State Health Insurance Assistance Program

The link to the website below provides you with a method of obtaining local help related to Medicare by offering you the ability to find the State Health Insurance Assistance Program which is specific to your state.

The State Health Insurance Assistance Programs (SHIP) are a national network of organizations whose mission is to "empower, educate, and assist Medicare-eligible individuals, their families, and caregivers through objective outreach, counseling, and training to make informed health insurance decisions that optimize access to care and benefits." The website is offered by the State Health Insurance Assistance Program National Technical Assistance Center. Although this is not a government organization, the State Health Insurance Assistance Programs for which it offers direct links and contact information through a "SHIP Locator" are all government programs. Furthermore, this website resource locator was developed with the partial support of a grant from the U.S. Department of Health and Human Services.

Basically, the purpose of this website is to give you an easy method to locate the official state government Medicare website of your choosing. All you have to do is to click the orange "SHIP Locator" button and select your state from the pop up menu. This will take you to a webpage which includes at least the phone number and the website of your official state government Medicare organization. This is exceedingly helpful if you want to find an official government online resource related to Medicare which happens to be specific to a certain state.

Chapter 5: What? You mean I still need more? Yes, you do.

Okay, so that was a ton of information. Maybe it feels like too much already. (Remember that you don't necessarily have to visit the resources listed in Chapter 4 unless you want more information; in many cases, the information and advice contained in this book (and specifically contained in Chapter 13 of this book) is enough.

But wait! There's more! More, you say? We just covered so much information already! How could there possibly be more to this subject?

Well, to be clear, the main content of this book deals with the four crucial layers of coverage you will need in order to receive adequate protection under the Medicare system. Let's remind ourselves again of what these four crucial layers consist of: Medicare Part A, Medicare Part B, Medicare Supplement Plans, and Prescription Drug Plans (PDPs).

A supplement? Why would I need that?

If you look back, we have technically covered only the first two of these essential layers, Medicare Part A and Medicare Part B. These two parts made up Original Medicare, the Medicare system which was originally in place before a few other parts and plans were added on.

So why were the additions to Original Medicare necessary? Am I saying that successfully enrolling in Original Medicare (which consists of Medicare Part A and Medicare Part B) is not enough?

Yes, that's exactly what I am saying.

Medicare Part A and Medicare Part B do not offer enough protection in terms of health care coverage for you. Simply put, Original Medicare is not enough.

Let us see why that is the case.

The Gaps, the Flaws, and the Flat-Out Gaping Holes which Exist in Original Medicare Coverage

Medicare Parts A and B (what you have signed up for if you have followed the enrollment procedures up to this point in the book) have a number of flaws and huge gaps in terms of the coverage that they offer to you.

So what are these gaps, the gaping holes in Medicare protection coverage? These flaws, gaps, and gaping holes consist of the coinsurance, the deductibles, the copays, and the cost/expense sharing amounts that are unlimited over the remainder of your life under Medicare. These gaps, flaws, and gaping holes in the Medicare coverage seriously limit the extent of the protection which is afforded to you by the Original Medicare program (Medicare Part A plus Medicare Part B).

Cost Sharing Potentially Gone Very, Very Wrong

There is currently no statutory limit on the aforementioned flawed cost sharing components of Medicare Part A and Medicare Part B. This means that there is the potential, the risk, for you to lose an extremely large quantity of money if you are enrolled in just Medicare Part A and Medicare Part B, Original Medicare, without having purchased any additional protection or coverage from a privately held insurance company.

In fact, a calculation which someone made not too long ago determined that in the worst case scenario possible (meaning that Murphy's law applies to the uttermost and that everything which can go wrong does indeed go wrong), a Medicare patient who was relying solely upon Original Medicare for his or her health coverage, upon Medicare Part A and Medicare Part B, could be liable for more than nine hundred thousand dollars in medical bills.

What?! How could a person who actually has health insurance be charged almost a million dollars in medical expenses for his or her treatment?

Well, the answer is: because of the gaps, the flaws, and the gaping holes in the coverage afforded to a person by original Medicare (Medicare Part A plus Medicare Part B). Those unlimited lifetime cost sharing elements can really add up.

So that is why you need other coverage beyond that which is provided by Medicare Part A and Medicare Part B. Here is where the insurance from a private company to serve as a much needed supplement to your Medicare coverage comes into play.

So What Do You Need to Do Now?

Well, first of all, if you have successfully enrolled in Medicare Part A and in Medicare Part B in that all important timely fashion which was described in detail in an earlier chapter, then you probably have some additional time to spare before your effective coverage date comes around. If this is the case, you can give yourself a small pat on the back and take a quick breather.

47

Go ahead and do something else for a little while—something fun or something else that has been on your mind—while you wait for your new Medicare Identification Card to arrive in the mail for you.

After a period of time spent waiting, you will at last receive your new Medicare identification card in your mailbox. This Medicare ID card will reveal to you what your unique "identifier" is (an alpha numeric string of digits which is also known as your Medicare Number). Your Medicare ID card will also clearly show to you the effective coverage start date for both Medicare Part A as well as Medicare Part B.

So you finally have your Medicare ID card. Now is the time to act. Now is the time to buy the extra supplemental private health insurance that will serve to protect you against those horribly treacherous flaws, gaps, and gaping holes in the coverage afforded to you by the Medicare program.

But what exactly should you buy? What are the types of insurance available to supplement your existing original Medicare (Medicare Part A plus Medicare Part B) coverage?

Types of Insurance Which Serve as a Supplement to Medicare

There are two basic kinds of insurance which have been made available to you in order to protect your finances from being utterly demolished and obliterated by Murphy's law and by those dangerous cost sharing elements in Medicare coverage. The two basic kinds of insurance are Medicare Supplement Plans (also commonly known as Medigap Plans) and Medicare Advantage Plans (also commonly known as Medicare Part C).

48

One of these types of insurance is quite obviously much better than the other type of insurance.

Medicare Supplement Plans—The Obviously Better Choice (and the Only Choice You Should Bother with!)

Medicare supplement plans constitute the best choice (and, quite frankly, the only choice if you are in your right mind) in terms of the type of health insurance you ought to buy in order to supplement your existing Medicare coverage. This type of supplemental coverage does assume that you will be able to afford the cost of a modest health insurance premium to be paid each month.

There are a range of Medicare supplement plans in existence. But due to the fact that the purpose of this book is to simplify a traditionally complicated and generally incomprehensible subject, I will recommend to you only the following few Medicare supplement plans:

For those of you who were eligible for Medicare before the year 2020, I can recommend to you either the super luxurious and comprehensive Plan F or the lower cost but still fairly high performance High Deductible Plan F (HDF).

For those of you who are first becoming eligible for Medicare in the year 2020 (meaning that you are reaching the age of 65 in the year 2020), neither Plan F nor the High Deductible Plan F (HDF) will be available to you, so I can recommend to you the following two Medicare supplement plans: the most luxurious, comprehensive Medicare supplement plan which will be available to you for purchase will be Plan G, and the Medicare supplement plan which will be the most cost effective option for you will be the High Deductible Plan G (HDG), a completely brand new type of plan.

Medicare Supplement Plans provide you with your much needed freedom of choice.

I will now take this opportunity to say this again in a clear and straightforward manner: Medicare Supplement Plans are the only way that you should go when it comes to purchasing a health insurance plan to cover the flaws and the gaps in your existing Medicare coverage. The only way, you hear me? THE ONLY WAY!

In fact, the following two chapters of this book will cover thoroughly all the reasons why I only ever recommend Medicare supplement plans to you in order to cover the gaps in the coverage you receive under original Medicare.

Medicare Advantage Plans (Part C)—The Type of Insurance Plan You Should Not Even Deign to Consider

Medicare Advantage Plans, also known as Medicare Part C, are trash. That is really the only definition you need to know for the purposes of this book. But I will give you just a little bit more in terms of the definition. After all, you have a right to know *why* these Medicare Advantage Plans (Part C) are just complete and utter garbage.

Medicare Advantage Plans (Part C) are a kind of supplemental insurance coverage which actually removes in their entirety the coverage you receive under Medicare Part A and under Medicare Part B, along with any and all of the protections and the benefits which they provide to you. Under these Medicare Advantage Plans (Part C), original Medicare (Medicare Part A plus Medicare Part B) is actually replaced in its entirety by a plan from an insurance company which confines any and all of its participants into a restrictive set of regulations, rules, and laws, similar to those which you might find in an HMO. It is basically like paying to lock yourself in a health care coverage prison.

So why on earth do you year so much about these trash Medicare Advantage Plans (Part C)? Well, the primary reason (and probably the only reason) is that the licensed insurance agent who sells one of these Medicare Advantage Plans to you gets paid an extremely generous commission through the brokerage of this plan, a commission which is largely derived from the blood, the sweat, and the tears of the taxpayer (you).

Just for the purposes of clarity, this book does discuss these Medicare Advantage Plans (Part C) in greater detail in Chapter 8. So if you have nothing better to do, you can take a gander at that chapter. After all, getting a better look at just how horrible these Medicare Advantage Plans (Part C) are will most likely boost your self-esteem and make you feel ever better and more superior for having made the smart, obvious choice of going with a Medicare Supplement Plan. You can read Chapter 8 to cement in your consciousness the fact that you've got at least one smart Medicare related decision under your belt.

Chapter 6: Medicare Supplement Plans— The Smart Choice (and Really, the Only Choice)

If you try to compare the Medicare Supplement Plans with the Medicare Advantage Plans (Part C), there is honestly no comparison, really. The Medicare Supplement Plans are vastly superior to the Medicare Advantage Plans (Part C) in almost every way. (This really shouldn't surprise you at all, since we have established that the Medicare Advantage Plans are basically complete trash pushed at you by the licensed insurance agents or brokers due to the obscenely high commissions they pay out to those people.)

However, there is one small way in which the Medicare Supplement Plans appear to be at somewhat of a disadvantage. And the small disadvantage is this: the Medicare Supplement plans are not given to you for free.

Each of the Medicare supplement plans carries with it a premium charge which is to be paid on a monthly basis. The exact costs of these plans, however, vary a great deal, depending on which state you reside in, from which insurance company you choose to purchase the Medicare supplement plan, and which kind of plan you choose to go with.

The Medicare supplement plans which are available to you for purchase are each denoted by one of the letters of the alphabet and have been standardized across the board. This means that no matter which private insurance company you choose to buy your Medicare supplement plan from, that plan will offer you exactly the same coverage as a plan of the same letter from a different private insurance company does.

Let us illustrate this with the following hypothetical example. Let us say there are two private insurance companies, Great Insurance Inc. and Super Insurance Inc. Both of these insurance companies offer a number of Medicare supplement plans. So Medicare Supplement Plan A when sold to you by Great Insurance Inc. will offer you exactly the same benefits, coverages, and protections as Medicare Supplement Plan A when it is sold to you by Super Insurance Inc. This fact applies *even if the two insurance companies are charging completely different prices for the same plan*.

Basically, if Great Insurance Inc. is charging a customer an insurance premium of four hundred dollars per month for Plan A, while Super Insurance Inc. has a premium price of a mere fifty-seven dollars per month for Plan A, it doesn't matter. The person paying four hundred dollars a month for Plan A is getting exactly the same coverage as the person who is paying fifty-seven dollars a month for Plan A. They are both Medicare Supplement Plan A, so both of these plans from totally different insurance companies sold at totally different prices will still provide you with the same exact coverage, benefits, and protections.

The price and the insurance company are, in a sense, immaterial, when it comes to Medicare supplement plans. The only thing that matters in terms of the coverage you are getting is what letter the plan is designated by.

So what is the moral of the story? Well, the moral of the story is that when you are purchasing a Medicare supplement plan, you can feel free to shop around for the best price, safe and secure in the knowledge that no matter which insurance company you end up buying your Medicare supplement plan from and no matter how low the price tag it comes with is, the coverage, benefits, and protections are standardized, identical across the board, as long as you are shopping for a plan denoted by a specific letter. Plan A will cover you in the same way no matter which insurance company you buy it from and no matter how much or how little you pay for it.

So, there are two primary reasons as to why you ought to go with one of the Medicare supplement plans as opposed to the Medicare Advantage Plans (Part C). And no, these reasons are not just that the Medicare Advantage plans (Part C) are complete and total trash. We will give some sound, logical reasons instead of merely trash talking, so here we go.

The two main reasons for choosing one of the Medicare supplement plans instead of the Medicare Advantage plans (Part C) are as follows: The first reason is that with the Medicare supplement plans, you get the freedom to choose whatever you want (as opposed to the completely restrictive rules and regulations of the Medicare Advantage plans (Part C)), and the second reason is that when you purchase a Medicare Supplement Plan, you will definitely get your money's worth (or even more than that).

Why you should go with a Medicare supplement plan: The freedom to choose

Currently, there are 12 types of Medicare Supplement plans which are available to be sold to the people who are eligible for Medicare. These 12 Medicare Supplement plans all have at least one fantastic attribute in common with one another: They provide you with the complete freedom to choose whatever you would like to choose. Let us now examine in more detail all the ways in which these Medicare Supplement plans offer you the complete freedom to choose whatever you want.

No Restriction in Terms of a Network of Hospitals and Doctors

First of all, Medicare supplement plans never restrict you to a particular network of doctors and/or a specific network of hospitals. A person who is covered by one of the Medicare supplement plans may choose to be seen and treated by any doctor or any hospital which accepts Medicare as a form of payment. This means that if you have a specific need for a particularly famous specialist, this doctor has not been placed beyond your reach by a restrictive list or a restrictive network of doctors or hospitals. If you need to see this particular specialist who is the best in the country, you can feel free to go to see him or her to be treated, as long as this specialist accepts Medicare as a form of payment.

No List of Which Providers or Doctors You Are Permitted to See

This benefit basically goes along with the first advantage. Because you can see any doctor or visit any provider you choose for your medical care due to the fact that there is no restrictive network of doctors, this means that you do not have to consult a list in order to determine exactly which provider you may go to for treatment. Furthermore, when you out of town, away from home, and you happen to need medical care or emergency treatment, you will not run the risk of experiencing any nasty financial surprises (like going to a doctor to be treated only to realize later on—when the medical bill comes—that the particular provider from whom you sought treatment is actually not part of your health insurance's approved network of providers). I dislike those books with the fine print and the nearly imperceptible and indiscernible pages of doctors and providers quite as much as the next person does.

Not Necessary to Request Any Permission from a Gate Keeper

The next benefit related to the freedom offered to you by one of the Medicare supplement plans could potentially save you a lot of time and a major headache. A person who is covered by one of the Medicare supplement plans is allowed to seek his or her treatment from any doctor or any specialist anywhere at any time (within the business hours of the provider, of course) without needing to request any permission at all from any kind of a gate keeper. This means that if you are experiencing a problem with the skin on your hands and you would like to see a dermatologist, there is no need for you to go first to your family physician in order to get a referral from him or her to go see a dermatologist. You can simply go straight to the dermatologist (as long as he or she accepts Medicare as a form of payment) to be seen directly by him or her, without any referral whatsoever.

Medicare Supplement Plans Are Valid Anywhere Within the Fifty United States and Its Possessions

These Medicare Supplement plans are good and valid throughout the entire United States, including its possessions. This is exactly how the parts of Original Medicare (Medicare Part A and Medicare Part B) function as well. Original Medicare and all the Medicare supplement plans may be used as a form of payment for treatment no matter which state or United States territory you happen to be in. (This can really help you out in the case of those emergency situations you may have every so often when you are travelling.)

As a side note and as an added benefit, the particular Medicare supplement plans which the previous chapter has already recommended to you (Plan F or the High Deductible Plan F for those who became eligible for Medicare before the year 2020 and Plan G or the High Deductible Plan G for those who become eligible for Medicare in the year 2020) all also possess an additional benefit of $50,000 for your lifetime for any emergency treatment which is undertaken in a foreign country.

Medicare Supplement Plans Are Guaranteed to Be Renewable and Will Continue to Offer the Same Benefits No Matter What

It is guaranteed that these Medicare Supplement plans will be renewable for the rest of your life. Also, whichever of these Medicare supplement plans you choose to go with will always continue to offer to you the exactly same level of coverage, protection, and benefits forever, as long as the insurance premium continues to be paid every month.

Even if you become ill with a critical, crippling, and debilitating illness, the coverage and the protection you receive under one of these Medicare supplement plans cannot be terminated or changed on you in any way. The private insurance company must uphold all its obligations related to your coverage, benefits, and protections, as long as you, the policy holder, fulfill your sole obligation, which is to pay the monthly premiums whenever they are due. As long as you, the customer, hold to your one obligation, the insurance company is required to uphold all of its obligations toward you, no matter how expensive it becomes for the insurance company to cover you.

A Word of Caution

Once the initial period of your guaranteed issue eligibility has gone by, if you try to apply to a different private insurance company or to apply for another type of plan, the insurance companies to which you are applying for new insurance might raise a question regarding your medical history. So when you are selecting your Medicare supplement plan and the private insurance company from which you will buy it, please do so with exceeding care. You may very well have that particular Medicare supplement plan for the remainder of your life.

But Exactly Which Medicare Supplement Plan Should You Buy?

Now that we have covered all the different ways in which each and every one of the Medicare supplement plans offers you the freedom of choice, which one of these twelve Medicare supplement plans should you actually choose to purchase?

The twelve Medicare supplement plans currently available are the following: Plan A, Plan B, Plan C, Plan D, Plan F, the High Deductible Plan F (HDF), Plan G, the High Deductible Plan G (HDG), Plan K, Plan L, Plan M, and Plan N.

Of course this list of Medicare supplement plans available for purchase comes with a few asterisks. The most important asterisk is the fact that Plan C, Plan F, and the High Deductible Plan F (HDF), are only available to you if you attained the age of eligibility for Medicare before the year 2020.

Now, please recall that the purpose of this book is to simplify an overly complicated subject. So, despite the many decent Medicare supplement plans available to you (all of which provide you with complete freedom of choice), I have already recommended to you only the following four Medicare supplement plans:

For those of you who were eligible for Medicare before the year 2020 (meaning that you reached the age of 65 in 2019 or earlier), I have already recommended to you either the super luxurious and comprehensive Plan F or the lower cost but still fairly high performance High Deductible Plan F (HDF).

For those of you who are first becoming eligible for Medicare in the year 2020 (meaning that you are reaching the age of 65 in the year 2020), neither Plan F nor the High Deductible Plan F (HDF) will be available to you, so I have already recommended to you the following two Medicare supplement plans: the most luxurious, comprehensive Medicare supplement plan which will be available to you for purchase will be Plan G, and the Medicare supplement plan which will be the most cost effective option for you will be the High Deductible Plan G (HDG), a completely brand new type of plan.

Now let us go into greater detail as to why I have recommended and continue to recommend these four particular Medicare supplement plans. The simple answer is this: You will get the most bang for your buck out of these four Medicare supplement plans.

Another reason why you should go with a Medicare supplement plan: Getting your money's worth

Essentially, with basically any Medicare supplement plan, you will get a great deal of bang for your fairly reasonably spent buck. But in particular, the Medicare supplement plans which will supply you the greatest amount of bang for the lowest and/or most reasonable level of buck are these four Medicare supplement plans: Plan F, the High Deductible Plan F (HDF), Plan G, and the High Deductible Plan G (HDG).

So exactly which of these supplement plans should you get?

The first set of plans I have recommended and continue to recommend to you provide you with the most protective, comprehensive, extensive health coverage which is allowed by the law. These two plans represent the Mercedes Benz of all Medicare supplement plans: Medicare Supplement Plan G and Medicare Supplement Plan F.

The second set of plans I have recommended and continue to recommend to you provide you with an excellent level of health coverage, protection, and benefits at an extremely low price. These two plans represent the Honda Accord (or the Toyota Camry—take your pick) of Medicare supplement plans, as they are extremely reliable, high performing, and reasonably affordable: Medicare Supplement High Deductible Plan G (HDG) and Medicare Supplement High Deductible Plan F (HDF).

Plan G

Medicare Supplement Plan G (also commonly known as Medigap Plan G) is for those who are attaining the age of 65 in the year 2020).

Plan F

Medicare Supplement Plan F (also commonly known as Medigap Plan F) is for those who attained the age of 65 before the year 2020).

High Deductible Plan G

Medicare Supplement High Deductible Plan G (also commonly known as Medigap High Deductible Plan G or HDG) is for those who are attaining the age of 65 in the year 2020).

High Deductible Plan F

Medicare Supplement High Deductible Plan F (also commonly known as Medigap High Deductible Plan F or HDF) is for those who attained the age of 65 before the year 2020).

More about All of These Plans: What Each One of Them Covers

Basically, Medicare Supplement Plan G along with Medicare Supplement High Deductible Plan G (HDG) are for those who turn 65 in the year 2020, and Medicare Supplement Plan F along with Medicare Supplement High Deductible Plan F (HDF) are for those who turned 65 in the year 2019 or earlier.

Every one of these four Medicare supplement plans covers the following costs in full, 100 percent of the way (with the exception of a Part B deductible where it has been noted below), fully covering and closing the various flaws, gaps, and gaping holes in the coverage under original Medicare (Medicare Part A and Medicare Part B):

The deductible for Medicare Part A
The coinsurance and the hospital costs for Medicare Part A
(up to an extra three hundred sixty five days after the benefits of Medicare have been used up)
The hospice care coinsurance or the hospice care copayment for Medicare Part A

The deductible for Medicare Part B – *Note: this is NOT covered under Medicare Supplement Plan G, nor is it covered under Medicare Supplement High Deductible Plan G (HDG)*
The coinsurance and the copayment for Medicare Part B
The excess charges for Medicare Part B

The coinsurance for a skilled nursing care facility

The cost of the first three pints of blood

All four of these plans also notably include coverage for the following:

80 percent coverage of any emergency expenses related to or incurred during travel in a foreign country (up to a total lifetime amount of $50,000) after the payment of a small deductible has been made

Even More about These Plans

Medicare Supplement Plan F carries with it no deductibles, no coinsurance, and no copays, nor does it carry any other kinds of cost sharing provisions or elements whatsoever. The person who is insured under Medicare Supplement Plan F will not be charged any money whatsoever or be sent any medical invoices for any routine, everyday cost sharing elements or expenses. Unfortunately, Medicare Supplement Plan F is not available to you if you reach the age of eligibility for Medicare in the year 2020 or later. Medicare Supplement Plan F is available to you only if you reached the age of eligibility for Medicare before the year 2020, that is, if you turned 65 in 2019 or earlier.

Medicare Supplement Plan G serves to reimburse those insured by it all of the money they pay for the above medical costs, aside from the Medicare Part B deductible, which comes to a total of $198 in the year 2020. Basically, Medicare Supplement Plan G covers everything that Medicare Supplement Plan F covers, except for the aforementioned Medicare Part B deductible.

Medicare Supplement High Deductible Plan F (HDF) and Medicare Supplement High Deductible Plan G (HDG) credit the amounts of the above medical expenses to their respective deductibles until each of those deductibles has been met. Once the deductible of a Medicare Supplement High Deductible Plan has been met, the High Deductible Plan will cover 100 percent of the rest of all the above medical costs and health care related expenses for the remainder of the year.

Allow me to tell you just a little bit more regarding the plans I most highly recommend, the Medicare Supplement High Deductible Plan F (HDF) and the Medicare Supplement High Deductible Plan G (HDG).

The simpler of these two Medicare Supplement High Deductible plans is, without a doubt, Medicare Supplement High Deductible Plan F (HDF). This, as you know by now, is available only to those who became eligible for Medicare before the year 2020.

The newer of these plans is the Medicare Supplement High Deductible Plan G (HDG). The Medicare Supplement High Deductible Plan G (HDG) will carry with it the same deductible as is carried by the Medicare Supplement High Deductible Plan F (HDF), and like the Medicare Supplement Plan G, it also will not credit the deductible for Medicare Part B in order to offset a portion of the deductible for the overall plan.

Basically, if you happen to be turning 65 years of age on January 1, 2020 or later, you will not be able to purchase any

Medicare Supplement plan at all which will cover the deductible for Medicare Part B. There are simply no plans available for you youngsters to do that. But there is no need to worry; the deductible for Medicare Part B is not an exceedingly unmanageable expense (for the year 2020, the total for this deductible will come to $198).

Each of the Medicare Supplement High Deductible Plans have become the unfortunate and undeserving bearers of a fairly scary and off putting name. After all, I know of no one who would want to willingly purchase a plan with "High Deductible" in the name—aside from you, smart reader, after having read this book and heard me sing the praises of these plans!

The name given to these Medicare Supplement High Deductible Plans is actually something of a misnomer. The high deductible for each of these plans is listed at $2,340. That, in itself, is a fairly off putting number. But again, the way these plans are named and presented is misleading. A person who is insured under the Medicare Supplement High Deductible Plan F (HDF) or under the Medicare Supplement High Deductible Plan G (HDG) will NOT be required to pay the starting $2,340 of their medical bills.

Rather, the person who is insured under either Medicare Supplement High Deductible Plan F (HDF) or Medicare Supplement High Deductible Plan G (HDG) will have to pay only the significantly lower deductibles for Medicare Part A and Medicare Part B (this depends on the kind of medical treatment they have to receive). After those small Medicare Part A and Medicare Part B deductibles have been paid, if the person insured under one of these High Deductible plans continues to receive medical treatment, then Medicare kicks in to pay for the vast majority of those medical bills.

The much smaller remainder of those medical invoices which is left over after Medicare has paid its significant majority is applied by the Medicare Supplement High Deductible Plan to the plan's deductible. Thus, the invoices which will be received by the person who is insured under Medicare Supplement High Deductible Plan F (HDF) or under Medicare Supplement High Deductible Plan G (HDG) will consist of the relatively low amounts left over from the medical expenses after Medicare has paid the lion's share of each of those medical expenses.

So what a person who is insured under Medicare Supplement High Deductible Plan F (HDF) or under Medicare Supplement High Deductible Plan G (HDG) will receive as a medical invoice from his or her health care provider is actually the relatively low amount of the medical expenses which were not already paid for by Medicare. And a person who is insured under one of these High Deductible plans has already been saving approximately one hundred dollars a month by forgoing the much more expensive and luxurious Medicare Supplement Plan F or Medicare Supplement Plan G. Since the person who is insured under Medicare Supplement High Deductible Plan F (HDF) or under Medicare Supplement High Deductible Plan G (HDG) is already saving over one thousand two hundred dollars per year on his or her monthly insurance premium, writing a check or two every now and then for a couple hundred bucks will not be too painful at all. The savings from the monthly premiums will generally outweigh the portion of the deductible which must be paid on these so called "High Deductible" plans.

Unless the person who is insured under Medicare Supplement High Deductible Plan F (HDF) or under Medicare Supplement High Deductible Plan G (HDG) is admitted to a hospital for an inpatient procedure, these medical invoices of low amounts will be for the 20 percent of any outpatient expenses which fall under the umbrella of Medicare Part B expenses. Medicare

Part B carries with it a yearly deductible of $198 (in the year 2020) and also a coinsurance cost of 20 percent of any of the treatment costs associated with Medicare Part B. Thus, a person who is covered by one of the high deductible plans will be required to pay 20 percent of these medical costs out of pocket in exchange for being able to save a substantial amount of money (approximately one thousand two hundred dollars per year) on his or her monthly insurance premiums.

The Bottom Line

Just as a recap of the most important points of this chapter:

In order to supplement the gaps, flaws, and gaping holes in the coverage you have under original Medicare (Medicare Part A and Medicare Part B), you should DEFINITELY purchase one of the twelve Medicare Supplement Plans (also commonly known as Medigap plans) instead of any of the Medicare Advantage Plans (Medicare Part C). This is due to the fact that all the Medicare Supplement plans offer you a complete level of freedom to choose. The Medicare supplement plans also offer you the greatest bang for your buck. The Medicare Advantage plans (Part C) are restrictive trash which eliminate the entirety of the coverage you receive under Original Medicare and which are only peddled to you so frequently due to the fact that each of these plans offer an obscenely high commission to the insurance broker or the insurance agent who manages to sell one of these trash plans to an unwitting customer. Don't be that person. Avoid the Medicare Advantage (Part C) Plans at all costs.

Instead, in order to supplement your coverage under Original Medicare (Medicare Part A and Medicare Part B), buy one of the Medicare Supplement Plans. The following four Medicare supplement plans deserve a particularly strong recommendation: Medicare Supplement Plan F, Medicare

Supplement Plan G, Medicare Supplement High Deductible Plan F (HDF), and Medicare Supplement High Deductible Plan G (HDG).

For those of you who were eligible for Medicare before the year 2020 (meaning that you reached the age of 65 in 2019 or earlier), I have already recommended to you either the super luxurious and comprehensive Plan F or the lower cost but still fairly high performance High Deductible Plan F (HDF).

For those of you who are first becoming eligible for Medicare in the year 2020 (meaning that you are reaching the age of 65 in the year 2020), neither Plan F nor the High Deductible Plan F (HDF) will be available to you, so I have already recommended to you the following two Medicare supplement plans: the most luxurious, comprehensive Medicare supplement plan which will be available to you for purchase will be Plan G, and the Medicare supplement plan which will be the most cost effective option for you will be the High Deductible Plan G (HDG), a completely brand new type of plan.

Medicare Supplement Plan F and Medicare Supplement Plan G are the most comprehensive plans available to you by law. Medicare Supplement Plan G covers everything that Medicare Supplement Plan F covers except for the deductible for Medicare Part B (which is $198 for the year 2020). These are luxurious and comprehensive plans with steeper monthly premiums, but they offer you the peace of mind that your medical expenses will be covered 100 percent of the way (aside from the $198 Medicare Part B deductible that does not get covered by Medicare Supplement Plan G).

Medicare Supplement High Deductible Plan F (HDF) and Medicare Supplement High Deductible Plan G (HDG) are a hidden secret, indeed, one of the best kept secrets in the world of all things related to Medicare and health care coverage. Medicare Supplement High Deductible Plan F (HDF) and Medicare Supplement High Deductible Plan G (HDG) offer excellent coverage at an exceedingly reasonable and low cost.

The name given to these Medicare Supplement High Deductible Plans is an utter misnomer. The high deductible for each of these plans is listed at $2,340. But a person who is insured under the Medicare Supplement High Deductible Plan F (HDF) or under the Medicare Supplement High Deductible Plan G (HDG) will NOT be required to pay the starting $2,340 of their medical bills. Instead, the person who is insured under the Medicare Supplement High Deductible Plan F (HDF) or under the Medicare Supplement High Deductible Plan G (HDG) will be required to pay only the much smaller deductibles of Medicare Part A and Medicare Part B, and if the medical treatment of the insured person continues, then Original Medicare (Medicare Part A and Medicare Part B) will kick in to pay the lion's share, the vast majority, of the insured person's medical bills.

So it is quite likely that a person insured under the Medicare Supplement High Deductible Plan F (HDF) or under the Medicare Supplement High Deductible Plan G (HDG) will be required to pay only a few hundred dollars of that $2,340 listed "high deductible." The insured person will likely pay only these few hundred dollars while saving approximately one thousand two hundred dollars a year on monthly premiums.

You do the math. The Medicare Supplement High Deductible Plan F (HDF) and the Medicare Supplement High Deductible Plan G (HDG) are clear winners in terms of a balance of medical coverage and money saving, in many situations and circumstances.

You know what? We are going to continue to belabor this point regarding the sheer awesomeness of High Deductible plans in the next chapter, Chapter 7. You won't believe how much of a misnomer the name "High Deductible Plan" is. The truth is that Medicare will actually be paying the vast majority of the medical benefits no matter which supplement plan you have in place (as long as there is indeed a Medicare supplement plan in place).

Chapter 7: Yes, you heard that right. High Deductible plans.

High deductible plans are, quite frankly, awesome. They are one of the best kept secrets in the whole system of health care and all things related to Medicare.

But you will be hard pressed to find a licensed insurance agent or a licensed insurance broker who would be willing to talk to you about these high deductible plans. Why won't they tell you openly about these plans? The fact of the matter is that these insurance agents would rather sell you a plan that is more expensive for you and which offers you poorer coverage but which pays them a nice and generous commission than to do the right thing and save you, the client, as much of your hard earned money as is possible while still providing you with a plan that offers you excellent coverage. Honestly, if the product the insurance agent or insurance broker gets you to buy is more expensive, then that insurance agent or insurance broker is making more money on commission. That is why insurance agents and insurance brokers are loathe to sell you decent, awesome products that will actually save you money—like these High Deductible plans.

It doesn't actually mean what you think it means

The name given to these Medicare Supplement High Deductible Plans is a complete and utter misnomer. The high deductible for each of these plans is listed at $2,340. And the paperwork which bears the official description of these Medicare Supplement High Deductible Plans is that each one carries with it a staggering $2,340 deductible which must be paid on an annual basis, implying that a person who is insured under one of these Medicare Supplement High Deductible Plans must first pay $2,340 out of pocket for his or her medical expenses in a year before Medicare and the supplemental health insurance coverage kick in to contribute even a single dime.

But the reality is that a person who is insured under the Medicare Supplement High Deductible Plan F (HDF) or under the Medicare Supplement High Deductible Plan G (HDG) will NOT be required to pay the starting $2,340 of their medical bills. The official description of the Medicare Supplement High Deductible Plan F (HDF) and the Medicare Supplement High Deductible Plan G (HDG) completely overlooks and/or flat out ignores the fact that original Medicare (Medicare Part A and Medicare Part B) will kick in to pay for the vast majority of the insured person's medical bills and expenses as soon as its miniscule deductible has been taken care of.

This is what actually happens and what the official brochures and the official documentation on the Medicare Supplement High Deductible Plan F (HDF) and the Medicare Supplement High Deductible Plan G (HDG) completely ignore:

The person who is insured under the Medicare Supplement High Deductible Plan F (HDF) or under the Medicare Supplement High Deductible Plan G (HDG) **WILL NOT BE REQUIRED TO PAY THE STARTING $2,340** of their medical bills but rather will be required to pay only the much smaller deductibles of Medicare Part A and Medicare Part B, and if the medical treatment of the insured person continues, then Original Medicare (Medicare Part A and Medicare Part B) will kick in to pay the lion's share, the vast majority, of the insured person's medical bills.

In the event of illness or injury, the person who is insured under the Medicare Supplement High Deductible Plan F (HDF) or under the Medicare Supplement High Deductible Plan G (HDG), after paying a small Medicare deductible, will pay a small percentage of the medical bills (while Medicare covers the lion's share of the insured person's medical expenses) until his or her small portion actually adds up to the deductible of the Medicare Supplement High Deductible Plan F (HDF) or the Medicare Supplement High Deductible Plan G (HDG). This deductible would likely only be reached in the case of an extremely bad year, health wise. But after that deductible is reached, the the Medicare Supplement High Deductible Plan F (HDF) or the Medicare Supplement High Deductible Plan G (HDG) pay out 100 percent of any further medical expenses.

The term "High Deductible plan" is a complete and total misnomer and is utterly misleading to the average consumer. In reality, the risk of incurring enough medical expenses so that the small percentage of those expenses actually ends up meeting the $2,340 plan deductible amount is fairly low. And the trade off benefit is huge. Each and every month, the Medicare Supplement High Deductible Plan F (HDF) or the Medicare Supplement High Deductible Plan G (HDG) could save you about one hundred dollars in monthly premiums when they are set in comparison to the premiums of the more luxurious Medicare Supplement Plan F and Medicare Supplement Plan G.

You may remember that several years ago, many people opted for a medical insurance plan which at first charged a small, manageable deductible. Then the insurance plan would enact a period of coinsurance or a period of cost sharing. And then, after the period of coinsurance or the period of cost sharing was over, the insurance plan would then at last begin to pick up and cover the cost of 100 percent of all remaining medical bills for the remainder of the year. For example, one such popular plan might be described to have a deductible of

$250, then an 80 percent 20 percent coinsurance cost sharing period of the next $5000 of medical expenses, and then a 100 percent time of coverage thereafter. This type of common and fairly popular medical insurance plan did a fairly decent job of protecting patients from medical bills which would be otherwise exceedingly painful and financially disastrous.

A wise buyer of a Medicare Supplement plan may opt to obtain a similar level of protection for a fairly meager insurance premium charge to be paid on a monthly basis. A person who is insured under the Medicare Supplement High Deductible Plan F (HDF) or under the Medicare Supplement High Deductible Plan G (HDG) will have a plan which may be described in the following manner: the plan will have a deductible of approximately $200 ($198 in the year 2020), then an 80 percent 20 percent cost sharing period for the next $10,000, and then receive full 100 percent coverage for the remainder of the year.

Who pays for what, exactly? And exactly when do the expenses get paid?

For a person who is insured under the Medicare Supplement High Deductible Plan F (HDF) or under the Medicare Supplement High Deductible Plan G (HDG), Medicare will actually begin covering 80 percent of all expenses related to outpatient care beginning immediately after the $198 Medicare Part B deductible is paid!

Here is what you and everyone thinking about Medicare related insurance needs to know about the Medicare Supplement High Deductible Plan F (HDF) and the Medicare Supplement High Deductible Plan G (HDG): **NO MATTER WHAT, MEDICARE WILL FIRST PAY ITS PORTION (WHICH JUST**

**SO HAPPENS TO BE THE LION'S SHARE) OF THE MEDICAL
BILLS. ALWAYS.**

Medicare actually does not know whether or not a Medicare
supplement plan is in place. It just begins to pay its 80 percent
lion's share of all medical bills related to outpatient care
(which, if you recall, is the portion taken care of by Medicare
Part B) after you pay the Medicare Part B deductible of $198.
For expenses related to Medicare Part A, which deals with
inpatient care and is usually more on the expensive side,
Medicare covers the cost of all of the charges from the
admitting hospital after the insured person pays a Medicare
Part A deductible of $1,408 (per hospital admission).

This means that after a fairly reasonable deductible has been
paid, Medicare will take care of 100 percent of all costs related
to having been admitted to a hospital. And Medicare will take
care of 80 percent of all costs related to outpatient care and
treatment after a small deductible of approximately $200 (or
$198 in the year 2020) has been paid. Amazingly, Medicare
does this (covering 100 percent of inpatient care expenses
after a deductible and covering 80 percent of outpatient care
expenses) even if there happens to be no Medicare
supplement plan in place whatsoever. In the worst case
scenario (in which an insured person undergoes a calamitous
series of disastrous medical occurrences), even the downside
risk of the Medicare Supplement High Deductible Plan F (HDF)
or the Medicare Supplement High Deductible Plan G (HDG) is
still quite reasonable.

Remember the Goal of This Book

Please take a moment to recall the audience for whom this
book has been written. This book is written for the average
person in need (or who will soon be in need) of Medicare. Just
to recap, for the purposes of this book, an *average* reader is a

person whose health is in an average condition or better, a person who possesses financial resources of an average amount or better, and a person who lacks any desire to waste one's valuable time and effort in studying and memorizing the minutia in regards to Medicare. Basically, for the purposes of this book, I am considering an average reader to be a person who is not destitute and who is not infirm or suffering from a debilitating disease. Thus, the average reader will most likely be well able to afford to pay the altogether reasonable and manageable premium price of the regular Medicare Supplement Plan F or of the regular Medicare Supplement Plan G, which, I would remind you, represent the Mercedes Benz of all Medicare supplement plans, as they offer the most comprehensive coverage available to you by law.

But no matter how comprehensive and protective the regular Medicare Supplement Plan F and the regular Medicare Supplement Plan G may be and no matter how reasonable and manageable their monthly premiums may be, the Medicare Supplement Plan F and the Medicare Supplement Plan G cannot be said to be the most cost effective choice when it comes to Medicare supplement plans. Indeed, without a doubt, the crown of cost effectiveness (while still maintaining an excellent and highly protective level of coverage) falls to the Medicare Supplement High Deductible Plan F (HDF) and the Medicare Supplement High Deductible Plan G (HDG).

Once you understand that the name "High Deductible Plan" is a complete utter misnomer, it is clear to see and compute the cost benefit analysis of this plan. Remember: A person who is insured under the Medicare Supplement High Deductible Plan F (HDF) or under the Medicare Supplement High Deductible Plan G (HDG) will have a plan which may be described in the following manner: the plan will have a deductible of approximately $200 ($198 in the year 2020), then an 80 percent 20 percent cost sharing period for the next $10,000, and then receive full 100 percent coverage for the remainder of the year.

In an average year, it is fairly unlikely that an average consumer will have outpatient medical bills which even come close to totaling $10,000. Thus, the person who is insured under the Medicare Supplement High Deductible Plan F (HDF) or under the Medicare Supplement High Deductible Plan G (HDG) will likely save around one thousand two hundred dollars per year (or perhaps more) when his or her premium costs are compared to the monthly premium costs of the luxurious and comprehensive Mercedes Benz plans, the Medicare Supplement Plan F and the Medicare Supplement Plan G.

Let us consider the possibility of a year that is not average. In fact, let us consider the possibility of a year in which Murphy's Law is out to get you and everything that could possibly go wrong does indeed go wrong, medically speaking. Surely, in the event of such a horrible, worst case scenario year, the luxurious and comprehensive Mercedes Benz plans, the Medicare Supplement Plan F and the Medicare Supplement Plan G, would serve as a better choice than the Medicare Supplement High Deductible Plan F (HDF) and the Medicare Supplement High Deductible Plan G (HDG). But actually, if you think through even this hypothetical worst case scenario, this is still not the case.

In the worst case scenario for a particular year, a person insured under the Medicare Supplement High Deductible Plan F (HDF) or under the Medicare Supplement High Deductible Plan G (HDG) will have to pay the entire deductible of $2,340 for his or her medical expenses during the year. This usually means that something tragic or disastrous, medically speaking, has occurred and the insured person has been admitted to the hospital, triggering Medicare Part A. Perhaps the person insured under the Medicare Supplement High Deductible Plan F (HDF) or under the Medicare Supplement High Deductible Plan G (HDG) has even been admitted to the hospital multiple times. And this insured person has also had to undergo a lot of outpatient treatment, triggering Medicare Part B as well. If all of these medically unfortunate occurrences happen to the insured person and he or she is admitted to the hospital several times and seen for outpatient procedures several more times, he or she will be required to pay out of pocket the entire $2,340 deductible for his or her High Deductible plan that year, since the costs of his or her hospital admittances and outpatient procedures have filled up the entirety of his or her deductible.

Okay, so in this worst case scenario, the insured person has to pay the full amount of the deductible for that year, the $2,340.

Let's take a moment to consider this.

This person who is insured under the Medicare Supplement High Deductible Plan F (HDF) or under the Medicare Supplement High Deductible Plan G (HDG) has already been saving one thousand two hundred dollars per year (or perhaps more) when his or her premium costs are compared to the monthly premium costs of the luxurious and comprehensive Mercedes Benz plans, the Medicare Supplement Plan F and the Medicare Supplement Plan G.

Thus, he or she can apply that savings of one thousand two hundred dollars per year to the $2,340 that he or she was forced to pay as a deductible due to this worst case scenario. $2,340 minus $1,200 is $1,140. This means that in terms of the out of pocket expense, he or she had to lay out a difference of $1,140 for that worst case scenario year, which is under $100 a month.

So in the worst case scenario, the luxurious and comprehensive Mercedes Benz plans, the Medicare Supplement Plan F and the Medicare Supplement Plan G, will offer you a savings of approximately $1,140 for that year.

But the Medicare Supplement High Deductible Plan F (HDF) and the Medicare Supplement High Deductible Plan G (HDG) already offer you a yearly savings of around $1,200!

So, unless you have a lot of worst case scenario years in succession (which is extremely unlikely), the Medicare Supplement High Deductible Plan F (HDF) and the Medicare Supplement High Deductible Plan G (HDG) will save you more money overall than the Medicare Supplement Plan F and the Medicare Supplement Plan G (because you would need the majority of your years to be worst case scenario years, medically speaking, in order to make the Medicare Supplement Plan F and the Medicare Supplement Plan G more cost effective than the Medicare Supplement High Deductible Plan F (HDF) and the Medicare Supplement High Deductible Plan G (HDG)).

The Bottom Line

You got it?

Unless you have several horrible years in a row in which medical disaster upon medical disaster occurs to you year after year, the Medicare Supplement High Deductible Plan F (HDF) and the Medicare Supplement High Deductible Plan G (HDG) are by far the most cost effective option. In fact, in order to make the Medicare Supplement Plan F and the Medicare Supplement Plan G more cost effective than the Medicare Supplement High Deductible Plan F (HDF) and the Medicare Supplement High Deductible Plan G (HDG), your bad or worst case scenario years in terms of medical care would actually need to outnumber your good or average years in terms of your medical care.

I understand. Sometimes you just want peace of mind, and you don't want to have to worry about incurring any unexpected medical bills. If this is the case, then the luxurious and comprehensive Mercedes Benz plans, the Medicare Supplement Plan F and the Medicare Supplement Plan G, will probably be a better fit for you. You will pay a fixed amount each month as a predictable, reasonable, and fairly manageable monthly insurance premium, and you will have no surprises, since 100 percent of your medical expenses will be covered by these Mercedes Benz plans.

But if you are choosing a Medicare Supplement plan based on cost and value and you want to save as much money as possible while getting as excellent of a coverage level as you can get, then go for the Medicare Supplement High Deductible Plan F (HDF) or the Medicare Supplement High Deductible Plan G (HDG). The money you save on monthly premium costs during average to good years medically speaking (which most of your years probably will be) will go straight into your pocket. CHA-CHING!

Chapter 8: Medicare Advantage Plans (Part C): Oh no you didn't!

Please don't. Just don't. Medicare Advantage Plans, also known as Medicare Part C, are not at all worth your time, your consideration, or your effort.

You know what? Just as the Medicare Supplement High Deductible Plan is a complete and total misnomer, the

Medicare Advantage Plan is also a misnomer. Perhaps an even worse misnomer. There is nothing at all advantageous about the poorly named Medicare "Advantage" plans (Part C).

In fact, there is actually only one good thing about the Medicare Advantage plans (Part C). This is the fact that they are extremely cheap to purchase. Oftentimes, the premiums on many of these Medicare Advantage plans (Part C) is actually zero dollars per month. Isn't that a good deal? Who doesn't love a freebie?

Well, there is no such thing as a free lunch. These Medicare Advantage plans (Part C) may actually be a decent deal if nothing bad ever happens to you and if you never ever need to go to the doctor or be admitted to the hospital. In other words, these Medicare Advantage plans (Part C) will suit you just fine until you actually require health insurance coverage.

Remember those licensed insurance agents and those licensed insurance brokers? They love these Medicare Advantage plans (Part C)! They promote these Medicare Advantage plans (Part C) extremely heavily to you, because every single time they sell one of these trash Medicare Advantage plans (Part C) to an unwitting customer, they receive an extremely generous and large commission. And those ridiculously generous commissions actually come on the backs of the American taxpayer.

So what else is there to know about these Medicare Advantage plans (Part C)? What are the flaws and the booby traps hidden in each one of these Medicare Advantage plans (Part C)? What are the pitfalls of which customers such as yourself ought to be made keenly aware?

Why you should NOT go with a Part C plan

Here are the primary reasons why you should definitely not go with a Medicare Advantage plan (Part C):

You can't choose! You're locked in!

When it comes to these Medicare Advantage plans (Part C), they are completely devoid of any freedom of choice whatsoever. You have no ability to choose, when you decide to go with one of these Medicare Advantage plans (Part C).

This is due to the fact that these Medicare Advantage plans (Part C) will be either PPOs (Preferred Provider Organizations) or HMOs (Health Maintenance Organizations). All of these types of plans rely on their own networks of hospitals and physicians to provide their customers with medical care. This means that you get the additional complication of having to limit yourself to a particular network of hospitals and doctors, and you have to select your health care provider from a list of names and locations in order to ensure that your medical treatment will in fact be covered by your health insurance provider.

Also, due to the fact that these networks of doctors and of hospitals are constantly changing and in flux because of certain physicians quitting that particular network and other physicians deciding to join that particular network, a person who has one of these Medicare Advantage plans (Part C) must constantly do comparison shopping year after year. If you finally find a doctor you like, but then that doctor decides to leave your network, you are no longer allowed to receive treatment from that doctor. You must instead find a replacement for him or her through the list which has been provided to you by your insurance company. Furthermore, if you have one of these Medicare Advantage plans (Part C) that includes coverage for prescription drugs, these plans are apt to change the formularies (the official lists which give the details of which medicines can be prescribed) they use fairly often, which will oftentimes render the entire plan significantly more expensive than it was before.

The Out of Pocket Costs of These Medicare Advantage Plans (Part C) Are Oftentimes Staggeringly High

Here is another horrible disadvantage of these Medicare Advantage plans (Part C). These Medicare Advantage plans (Part C) have an average out of pocket deductible limit of more than five thousand dollars per year. Some of these Medicare Advantage plans (Part C) even have an out of pocket deductible limit that reaches six thousand seven hundred dollars! Why on earth would you shun a "High Deductible" plan that carries with it an out of pocket deductible limit of $2,340 and at the same time somehow be comfortable with a potential out of pocket deductible loss of six thousand seven hundred dollars? It really makes no sense. No sense at all. If a customer is willing to swallow a deductible of five thousand dollars or even of six thousand seven hundred dollars, he or she should be more than willing to put up with a supposedly "high deductible" of $2,340.

The Hidden Fees of These Medicare Advantage Plans (Part C) Can Also Add Up

Even the most popular of these Medicare Advantage plans (Part C) can bludgeon to death a person they are insuring with ridiculous copays and hidden fees for just about everything. Here is a brief sampling of one of these Medicare Advantage plans (Part C), which is actually one of the best selling plans in Florida. The copays and hidden fees for this Floridian Medicare Advantage (Part C) plan are as follows:

A hospital stay will cost you $175 per day for the first ten days.

An ambulance will cost you $300.
The supplies used to treat diabetes will come with a 20 percent coinsurance cost.
The lab services will cost you $100 per day.
The diagnostic radiology will cost you up to $125 as a copay.
The therapeutic radiology will cost you a copay of $35 or up to 20 percent of the cost.
The outpatient X-rays will cost you up to $100 per day.
The renal dialysis will cost you 20 percent of the actual cost for the treatment.

I don't know about you, but I think that's insane. Willingly subjecting yourself to that high of a deductible and to that many hidden fees and copays is pretty insane, especially when you consider what a good deal those Medicare Supplement plans are and what decent, comprehensive coverage they provide. Even the higher, more expensive monthly premiums for the luxurious and comprehensive Mercedes Benz plans, the Medicare Supplement Plan F and the Medicare Supplement Plan G, are dwarfed by just a few of these fees, copays, and deductibles!

These Medicare Advantage Plans (Part C) Present a Great Risk for Costly Complications

These Medicare Advantage plans (Part C) can result in a number of potentially costly and financially disastrous complications. For instance, if you are undergoing surgery, you may have made sure that the surgeon who performs your surgery is within the approved network of doctors, but it is possible that he or she works with an anesthesiologist who is not in the network approved by your insurance company. Or the radiologist you see may be part of your approved health insurance network, but the persons who read and analyze the films might not be part of that network. In such a case, you would be slapped with one or two huge medical bills that are not at all defrayed or covered by your trashy health insurance plan.

You May Have to Go Through a Gate Keeper to Get Permission

Oftentimes, these Medicare Advantage plans (Part C) will require you to first seek permission or a referral from your regular doctor in order to seek medical treatment from a specialist. For instance, if you are suffering from a skin problem on your hands and you need to see a dermatologist right away, you will probably not be able to do so, since you will probably need to contact your insurance company to get permission first and also go to your regular doctor in order to receive a referral to a dermatology specialist.

The Networks for These Medicare Advantage Plans (Part C) Are Oftentimes Geographically Quite Restricted

The networks for these Medicare Advantage plans (Part C) oftentimes operate locally and are restricted to a particular geographical area, which means that if you want or need to receive medical treatment when you are out of town, traveling, or living in a second home, this can cause a huge headache and can prevent you from receiving the medical treatment you require in a timely manner.

These Medicare Advantage Plans (Part C) Make Promises Which They Are Loathe to Keep

These Medicare Advantage plans (Part C) may promise that they will cover any emergency care which is out of their network, but, when it comes time to reimburse you for your expenses or to pay the actual medical invoices, these

Medicare Advantage plans (Part C) may balk at actually covering and paying for those promised costs.

Those Licensed Insurance Agents Are Not Always So Forthcoming

The licensed insurance agents who try their best to enroll you in one of these Medicare Advantage plans (Part C) by tempting you with the fact that the monthly premiums are "free" or "low cost" may then bludgeon you into also purchasing added Hospital Indemnity insurance which is supposed to pay for the hidden fees and costs which are not covered by these Medicare Advantage plans (Part C).

The Extras of These Medicare Advantage Plans (Part C) Are Oftentimes Half Baked

These Medicare Advantage plans (Part C) will oftentimes tout a number of seemingly lucrative extras, such as vision, hearing, and dental coverage. Unfortunately, these extras are generally discount plans which offer disappointingly limited and restricted benefits instead of genuine insurance coverage. Also, these extras usually rely on tiny networks of dentists and doctors, which further limits the freedom of choice of the customer.

Well, if you really want to go ahead and spend your hard-earned money, I guess I can't stop you...

Here is a principle that may sound a bit cliched but which definitely rings true here, in the case of these Medicare Advantage plans (Part C): You get what you pay for.

The only way a private insurance company would be willing to give away one of its products for free is if someone is picking up the slack and paying for it. In this case, the United States government (and, in effect, you, the American taxpayer) bears the brunt of the cost burden for these seemingly "free" or "low cost" health insurance plans. As soon as the government chooses to cut down on some of its expenses, the taxpayers and the insurance customers will be those who will have to take up the slack and bear the brunt of the burden. And of course, these plans will be promoted all the while by those licensed insurance agents, touted and sold to you as if their lives hang in the balance.

The Silver Lining

If you are currently a victim of one of these Medicare Advantage plans (Part C), there is still hope for you, a silver lining amidst the otherwise impossibly dark and gloomy Medicare Advantage clouds.

The silver lining is this: it is not too late for you to switch health insurance plans. Those who are holders of these Medicare Advantage plans (Part C) are permitted to change to a different plan and/or a different insurance company each year during the Medicare Annual Election Period (AEP) or during the Open Enrollment Period (OEP). These designated periods are intended to enable dissatisfied customers like you to switch to a new plan which will take effect on the first day of the following calendar year.

The Bottom Line

I would not recommend these Medicare Advantage plans (Part C) to anyone, unless you are so destitute that you cannot afford a monthly premium payment of even $50. And if you are destitute and do in fact resort to one of these Medicare Advantage plans (Part C), you will need to do your best to make sure that you rarely ever require medical attention, because if you are forced to seek medical treatment, the high out of pocket deductibles, the ridiculous copays, and the hidden fees and costly complications on just about everything will serve to make you even more destitute than you were before.

So basically, I do not recommend these Medicare Advantage plans (Part C) to anyone. As was mentioned earlier on several occasions, these Medicare Advantage plans (Part C) are just trash. Essentially worthless in pretty much every way that might matter to anyone.

Chapter 9: Part D: The Drugs

Okay. So we have now gone over three out of the four essentials layers for coverage under the Medicare program.

We have covered both Medicare Part A and Medicare Part B, the two components of original Medicare.

We have gone over the various benefits of Medicare Supplement Plans and discussed which Medicare Supplement plans you ought to purchase (such as the luxurious, comprehensive Mercedes Benz-style plans, the Medicare Supplement Plan F and the Medicare Supplement Plan G, or the extremely cost effective but still high performing Honda Accord/Toyota Camry-style plans, the Medicare Supplement High Deductible Plan F (HDF) and the Medicare Supplement High Deductible Plan G (HDG).

And we have also covered in great detail all the reasons why those Medicare Advantage plans (Part C) ought to be avoided at all costs (like the plague or like a big stinky pile of garbage).

So just to recap, the four layers of health insurance coverage which are necessary for adequate protection under the Medicare system consist of precisely the following four items:

- Medicare Part A
- Medicare Part B
- Medicare Supplement Plans
- Prescription Drug Plans (PDPs)

We have gone over the first three layers in more than sufficient detail. Now it is time to take a look at the last crucial layer for adequate protection under the Medicare system. This is the Prescription Drug Plan, or PDP, also known as Medicare Part D.

Why you need a Prescription Drug Plan (PDP)

The federal government, in its boundless generosity, now helps to subsidize the expense of the prescription drug plans (PDPs) which may be purchased from a private insurance company. Each one of these private insurance companies is allowed to price the drug plans it offers however it wants to, to compile its own list of the drugs which are to be covered (these lists are known as formularies) and to offer differing levels of benefits to its customers.

Unfortunately, this structure has caused a number of problems to arise. The first problem is that the structure of each prescription drug plan (PDP) looks exceedingly complicated to anyone who is not an insurance professional. Such prescription drug plans (PDPs) include deductibles, coinsurance, copays, and a big donut hole.

In addition, the insurance premiums and the formularies of each prescription drug plan (PDP) may change from one year to the next year. Also, the prescription medication required by a person can of course change from time to time.

What then should be done regarding a prescription drug plan (PDP)? This is what you should do: You should compare all the available prescription drug plans (PDPs) and choose one solely on the basis of its estimated out of pocket cost every year.

If the change in the prescription drug plan's formulary, drug, or premium cost warrant a reconsideration of your prescription drug plan (PDP), then you as the insured person are able to select a new prescription drug plan (PDP) from a new insurance company at the time of the yearly open enrollment period (OEP) for the next year.

A relatively painless way to compare the prices of every single prescription drug plan (PDP) in your area exists through the government website. The step by step directions to navigate this comparison are listed down below.

If you are blessed with such health that you have no need of prescription drugs whatsoever, consider your future. Do you think there may be a need to insure yourself against potentially high prescription drug costs at any point in the future? If there is not and you expect that you will never need to purchase one of these prescription drug plans (PDPs), then congratulations. You are completely done with your enrollment in the Medicare system and all things related to it.

On the other hand, many other people who cannot see so clearly into the future prefer to be able to keep their options open and avoid the possibility of a lifetime penalty that comes with late enrollment.

If a customer becomes eligible for buying a prescription drug plan (PDP) but chooses not to do so and then instead chooses to buy a prescription drug plan (PDP) at a later point in time sometime in the future, a late enrollment penalty that will last your entire lifetime is assessed for every single month which elapsed from the time of the customer's initial eligibility to the time of the actual purchase of the prescription drug plan (PDP).

This lifetime late enrollment penalty equates to approximately 35 cents a month for every month which has elapsed. This means that a three year delay in enrollment will translate to a late enrollment penalty of $12.60 a month for the rest of your life.

So unless you are really sure that you will never ever need to take any prescription drugs for the rest of your life, you should buy at the very least a cheaper prescription drug plan (PDP) from the time at which you are initially eligible (even if you are not yet taking any prescription drugs). These cheaper prescription drug plans (PDPs) may cost you around $13 a month.

A step-by-step guide to choosing the prescription drug plan (PDP) that saves you the most money

Step 1

Visit the following website: https://www.medicare.gov/plan-compare/

Step 2

Click on the "Continue without logging in" button

Step 3

Click on the "Drug Plan (Part D)" button

Step 4

Type in your zip code and click on the "Select Your Location" button

Step 5

Click on the "I don't get help from any of these programs" button

Step 6

Click on the "Yes" button (you wish to see the costs of the drugs as you are comparing the plans)

Step 7

Choose the way you prefer to fill your prescriptions (by mail order, at the retail drug store, or both)

Step 8

Add the prescription drugs you are taking: type in each of the drugs on your list and click on the "Add Drug" button as soon as it becomes green

Step 9

Add the information about each of the prescription drugs on your list. Click on the "Add Drug to My List" button before you start a new drug entry

Step 10

Click on the "Done Adding Drugs" button once all of your prescription drugs have made it onto the list

Step 11

Choose one to three of the drug stores you like best, even if you are going to utilize mail order exclusively; click on the "Done" button

Step 12

The next page will include a list of all the available prescription drug plans (PDPs) in your location. Use the default sort function in the upper right hand corner to sort the list by "Lowest monthly premium"

Step 13

This is critical: change it to "Lowest Drug + Premium Cost" by using the drop down menu

Step 14

Look at plans on the list

Step 15

Click on the "Add to compare" button for two or three of the plans and then click on the "Compare" button in order to navigate to the comparison page

Step 16

Decide which plan you wish to purchase; I would recommend that the total annual cost serve as the basis for your decision

Step 17

Click on the "Enroll" button to purchase the plan

Helpful Hints

Your existing prescription drug plan (PDP), if you have one, will be automatically cancelled as soon as the application for a new prescription drug plan (PDP) is accepted.

You may change your prescription drug plan (PDP) in the fall if you so choose.

Find the plan which will offer you the lowest total annual cost, according to the prescriptions you currently take and your favorite locations to fill those prescriptions.

If you followed the directions well, then the cheapest plan ought to top the list. Use the "Enroll" button to enroll.

You may wish to repeat this process every year during the Annual Enrollment Period (AEP) in order to check that you still have the plan with the lowest cost.

Chapter 10: So how much will I actually have to pay?

Obviously, the insurance coverage you obtain will (and ought to) cost you something. Let us take a look to see how much your insurance will cost you.

What exactly is IRMAA, and why do I care?

IRMAA, or Income Related Monthly Adjustment Amount, is known as the success penalty. IRMAA can add on to the premium you pay monthly for Medicare Part B as well as for your prescription drug plan (PDP), depending on what your Modified Adjusted Gross Income (MAGI) was two years before as recorded by the IRS.

The IRMAA tables will usually change from year to year. You can find these tables online.

2020 Medicare Likely Monthly Premium Costs by Plan

The intended audience for this book will likely encounter these 2020 premium costs on a monthly basis:

Medicare Part A
Free of Charge (after forty quarters of taxable earnings)

Medicare Part B
$144.60 (This could be substantially increased by IRMAA)

Medicare Supplement Plans: the premiums for these will vary based on a number of factors, including the state of residence, sex, age, zip code, and possibly smoking status

High Deductible Plan F
Around $30 to $80 (this is the most cost effective)

High Deductible Plan G
A little less than HDF (similarly cost effective)

Plan F
Around $140 to $250 (this is the most comprehensive plan available)

Plan G
A little less than that of Plan F due to the fact that it does not cover the Part B deductible

Prescription Drug Plan (PDP)
$13 or more (depends on location, plan, drug deductibles, coinsurance, and copay. May also be affected by IRMAA)

2020 Medicare Provisions for Cost Sharing

Part A
Deductible and coinsurance are payable by either you or your Medicare supplement
Deductible for each hospital admission: You must pay $1,408
Coinsurance for hospital days 1 through 60: You must pay $0
Coinsurance for hospital days 61 through 90: You must pay $352 per day
Coinsurance for lifetime reserve days 91 through 150: You must pay $704 per day

Skilled Nursing Facility:
Coinsurance days 0 through 20: You must pay $0
Coinsurance days 21 through 100: You must pay $176 per day

Part B
Deductible (annual): $198
Coinsurance (without limit): 20 percent

Chapter 11: Medicare Supplement Plans by Massachusetts, Minnesota, and Wisconsin

This chapter is dedicated to the three states which somehow persuaded the United States federal government to grant them waivers which allow each of the states to generate its own set of Medicare Supplement plans. These outlier Medicare Supplement plans are still all far superior to the Medicare Advantage plans (Part C). For instance, all of these states' Medicare Supplement plans will function anywhere within the United States, and none of them possess a restrictive network of doctors and hospitals.

Massachusetts

Massachusetts has made the following two plans available: the Core Plan and the Supplement 1 Plan. The basic benefits for each of these plans are the same, and they also include additional components to fill the holes found in Original Medicare in addition to some benefits which are mandated by the state.

The Core Plan is leaner and less costly than the Supplement 1 Plan. Get the Core plan if you wish to save money. Or you can perform a more detailed analysis involving the perusal of the added benefits of the Supplement Plan 1 to see if those extra benefits would be worthwhile for your needs.

Minnesota

Minnesota offers a wide variety of Medicare Supplement plans: Basic, Basic + optional riders, Extended Basic, and the Medicare Supplement Plans High Deductible Plan F, Plan K, Plan L, Plan M, and Plan N. There are some basic benefits which are shared by both the Basic and the Extended Basic plans.

You may want to consider the optional riders, which could potentially allow you to create a plan that covers every potential risk. But of course, for the sake of simplicity, you can just try to get High Deductible Plan F.

Wisconsin

Wisconsin offers a build-your-own take on Medicare Supplement plans. It offers Basic Benefits, and to these you can add more Optional Riders to achieve the desired level of coverage.

You ought to consider the High Deductible plan with the deductible of $2000. This option may provide you with the most bang for your buck.

Chapter 12: Oops! You chose the wrong plan before reading this book? You're paying too much? Never fear!

If you had no idea about Medicare Supplement Plans and fell victim to a Medicare Advantage plan (Part C), there is still hope for you.

Also, if you have a Medicare Supplement plan that is not lettered "F" or "G" but you have seen the light and wish to sign up for one of the more highly recommended Medicare supplement plans, such as the luxurious, comprehensive Mercedes Benz-style plans, the Medicare Supplement Plan F and the Medicare Supplement Plan G, or the extremely cost effective but still high performing Honda Accord/Toyota Camry-style plans, the Medicare Supplement High Deductible Plan F (HDF) and the Medicare Supplement High Deductible Plan G (HDG), then there is also still some hope for you.

What can you do?

To you who are repenting, I will be the bearer of both good news as well as bad news.

The good news is this:

If you are currently a victim of one of those horrid Medicare Advantage plans (Part C), it is not the end of the world. It is not too late for you to switch to a different health insurance plan. Those who are holders of these Medicare Advantage plans (Part C) are permitted to change to a different plan and/or a different insurance company each year during the

Medicare Annual Election Period (AEP) or during the Open Enrollment Period (OEP). These designated periods are intended to enable dissatisfied customers like you to switch to a new plan which will take effect on the first day of the following calendar year.

Here is some other good news:

If you have not fallen victim to one of those Medicare Advantage plans (Part C) but you wish to switch to one of the Medicare supplement plans which have been recommended to you in this book, like the luxurious, comprehensive Mercedes Benz-style plans (the Medicare Supplement Plan F and the Medicare Supplement Plan G) or the extremely cost effective but still high performing Honda Accord/Toyota Camry-style plans (the Medicare Supplement High Deductible Plan F (HDF) and the Medicare Supplement High Deductible Plan G (HDG)), then you are allowed to apply for one of these Medicare supplement plans whenever it strikes your fancy.

But here is the bad news:

Once your initial enrollment period has passed (which happens just a few months after you become eligible for Medicare), there is no longer any period of "guaranteed issue" for these Medicare Supplement plans. This means that in attempting to change plans, the insurance company might ask you a list of detailed questions regarding your medical history to ensure that you are in fact insurable. So basically, if you are past your initial enrollment period, there may be some (or several) hoops through which you need to jump in order to be able to purchase a Medicare Supplement plan beyond your initial enrollment period. You run the risk of being refused if your medical history and your medical condition are too low for the insurability standards of that insurance company.

Chapter 13: A Step-by-Step Guide and Summary of Everything You Need to Know and Do (aka the Only Chapter You Actually Care About)

Follow these steps to get all the coverage you will ever need related to Medicare. If you need more information, you can refer to the relevant section toward the end of this chapter.

Step 1: Choose an Appropriate Medicare Part A and Part B Start Date

Read more below if you want to know how to choose the right start dates.

Where to Enroll

It is actually surprisingly easy to enroll in both Medicare Part A and Medicare Part B. In fact, the entire process of enrollment in Medicare Part A using the following website may even take you as little as or perhaps even fewer than ten minutes in total.

The link directly below is where you can go online in order to enroll yourself in Medicare Part A and Medicare Part B; the website is quite user-friendly and for the most part self-explanatory:

https://www.ssa.gov/medicare/

Also, please do not be bothered at all if the above link happens to redirect you to the following link:

https://www.ssa.gov/benefits/medicare/

Both of these links link to exactly the same website (the one through which you can apply for Medicare Part A and Medicare Part B as easily and as painlessly as possible).

Step 2: Get in Touch with a Licensed Insurance Agent and Choose and Apply for a Medicare Supplement Plan; Make Sure the Effective Coverage Date Is the Same as That of Medicare Part B

Below are descriptions of the supplement plans which are most highly recommended. See the end of this chapter for a more detailed description.

The right supplement plan for you

These are the Mercedes Benz of all Medicare Supplement Plans. They offer to you the most comprehensive coverage available by law.

They are best for those who are risk averse, who possess a comfortable financial situation, and who want their medical expenses to be 100 percent covered no matter how much it costs.

Plan F
This is the most popular choice and comes with the highest monthly insurance premium but offers the most comprehensive structure of benefits. It covers 100 percent of all copays, deductibles, and coinsurance. If the treatment is Medicare approved, you will never be charged. Only available to those who turned 65 years of age before the year 2020.

Plan G
This will no doubt become the most popular choice and comes with one of the highest monthly insurance premium but offers the most comprehensive structure of benefits aside from that of Plan F. It covers 100 percent of what Plan F covers, with the exception of the $198 Part B deductible. Available to those who turn 65 years of age in the year 2020 or later.

These are the Honda Accords or the Toyota Camrys of the Medicare Supplement plans. They are the most cost effective forms of coverage and still offer excellent performance and protection.

These plans are suited to those who want a lower monthly premium and are willing to assume some risk and some cost sharing elements.

High Deductible Plan F
Covers everything that Plan F above covers, but pays a bit less than 100 percent (80 percent) from the first day of the year (cost sharing structure).

High Deductible Plan G
Covers everything that Plan G above covers, but pays a bit less than 100 percent (80 percent) from the first day of the year (cost sharing structure).

Step 3: Choose a PDP

A step-by-step guide for choosing the least expensive PDP

Step 1

Visit the following website: https://www.medicare.gov/plan-compare/

Step 2

Click on the "Continue without logging in" button

Step 3

Click on the "Drug Plan (Part D)" button

Step 4

Type in your zip code and click on the "Select Your Location" button

Step 5

Click on the "I don't get help from any of these programs" button

Step 6

Click on the "Yes" button (you wish to see the costs of the drugs as you are comparing the plans)

Step 7

Choose the way you prefer to fill your prescriptions (by mail order, at the retail drug store, or both)

Step 8

Add the prescription drugs you are taking: type in each of the drugs on your list and click on the "Add Drug" button as soon as it becomes green

Step 9

Add the information about each of the prescription drugs on your list. Click on the "Add Drug to My List" button before you start a new drug entry

Step 10

Click on the "Done Adding Drugs" button once all of your prescription drugs have made it onto the list

Step 11

Choose one to three of the drug stores you like best, even if you are going to utilize mail order exclusively; click on the "Done" button

Step 12

The next page will include a list of all the available prescription drug plans (PDPs) in your location. Use the default sort function in the upper right hand corner to sort the list by "Lowest monthly premium"

Step 13

This is critical: change it to "Lowest Drug + Premium Cost" by using the drop down menu

Step 14

Look at plans on the list

Step 15

Click on the "Add to compare" button for two or three of the plans and then click on the "Compare" button in order to navigate to the comparison page

Step 16

Decide which plan you wish to purchase; I would recommend that the total annual cost serve as the basis for your decision

Step 17

Click on the "Enroll" button to purchase the plan

Helpful Hints

Your existing prescription drug plan (PDP), if you have one, will be automatically cancelled as soon as the application for a new prescription drug plan (PDP) is accepted.

You may change your prescription drug plan (PDP) in the fall if you so choose.

Find the plan which will offer you the lowest total annual cost, according to the prescriptions you currently take and your favorite locations to fill those prescriptions.

If you followed the directions well, then the cheapest plan ought to top the list. Use the "Enroll" button to enroll.

You may wish to repeat this process every year during the Annual Enrollment Period (AEP) in order to check that you still have the plan with the lowest cost.

More Information

From Chapter 3:

Medicare Part A is the health insurance which is offered by the United States federal government to those Americans who have reached the age of 65 or older. Medicare Part A is designed to reimburse to those who are covered by it a portion of or, ideally, all of the costs which are incurred during the treatment of a patient in inpatient facilities such as a hospital, a rehabilitation facility, and a skilled nursing care facility.

In almost every case, an American who has worked in the United States for ten or more years (or who is married to a person who has worked in the United States for ten or more years) and who has paid taxes on that employment will get Medicare Part A offered to him or her free of charge, with no cost whatsoever.

Due to the fact that Medicare Part A is free of charge, basically everyone is supposed to have enrolled in Medicare Part A by the time they reach their 65th birthday.

The coverage effective date, or the date on which a person's Medicare Part A coverage takes effect (as is the case with all coverages which are related to Medicare) always falls on the first day of the month in question.

Almost all of the time, a person who is about to reach the age of 65 may choose to enroll in Medicare Part A up to 3 months before the start of his or her birthday month. If a person chooses to apply early in this fashion, the coverage he or she will receive under Medicare Part A will take effect on the very first day of his or her birthday month (and not on the first day of the month in which he or she enrolled, if he or she chose to enroll in Medicare Part A before his or her birthday month came around).

In addition to the three month period of early enrollment in Medicare Part A, a person also has available to them the possibility of enrolling in Medicare Part A for a few months after his or her birth month has passed. However, enrolling late in this manner might possibly mean that the person must be without coverage by his or her health insurance during this period of time.

Note 1: This an exception to one of the above rules. If a person's actual date of birth happens to fall on the first of any month, his or her coverage under Medicare Part A (and under any other coverage associated with or related to Medicare) will take effect on the very first day of the month prior to his or her birthday month. You can try to ask what the reason for this is, but honestly, it is pretty likely that no one has any idea why this might be the case.

Note 2: This is a second exception, this time relating to the timeline related to a person's enrollment in Medicare Part A. If a person has an existing health insurance policy that is a Health Savings Account (HSA) and he or she wishes to continue to offer pre-tax contributions, he or she may want to consult with an expert regarding the delaying of his or her enrollment in Medicare Part A, since the coverage offered by Medicare Part A might preclude deductible contributions to an HSA plan.

From Chapter 4:

Medicare Part B is the health insurance which is offered by the United States federal government to those Americans who have reached the age of 65 or older. Medicare Part B is usually designed to reimburse to those who are covered by it a portion of or, ideally, all of the costs which may be incurred during the treatment by a doctor or doctors of a patient in an outpatient capacity such as in a doctor's office, etc. as well as the expenses which may be incurred for testing and diagnostics, medical supplies, medical equipment, and preventative health care.

Recall that outpatient care relates to treatment which a patient receives without needing to be admitted to a hospital, a skilled nursing care facility, etc. Thus, Medicare Part B generally deals with the coverage for health care that is more on the routine side and is usually less severe.

The Timing Surrounding Your Enrollment in Medicare Part B

It is of vital importance that you know to select the effective date of the coverage which you receive under Medicare Part B with great care. This is the reason why: Medicare Part B comes at a substantial monthly cost. The monthly premium for Medicare Part B in the year 2020 starts at $144.60 per month. Because of this substantial cost, it would not be considered wise to start your coverage under Medicare Part B at too early of a time. If you decide to start Medicare Part B too early, you may end up paying a lot more than you ought to for your Medicare related health coverage.

On the other hand, due to the fact that Medicare Part B is a crucial layer of protection which is intended to reimburse you for the expenses incurred during those treatments which are most frequently encountered, it would be considered **exceedingly unwise** for you to start your coverage under Medicare Part B too late.

If one waits too long after he or she becomes eligible and chooses to enroll too late for Medicare Part B, he or she runs the risk of incurring hefty, staggering medical bills with zero protection from health insurance to help to defray the cost. Furthermore, if a person fails to enroll for Medicare Part B

111

until the period of eligibility has passed entirely, then the opportunity for him or her to enroll in Medicare Part B will then be limited to just a brief period of time at the start of each of the following years, and the coverage received through this late enrollment in Medicare Part B will fail to take effect for a number of months after the late enrollment takes place.

In addition to that, any enrollment in Medicare Part B which may be considered substantially late will subject the person who enrolled late to a monetary penalty which will literally last a lifetime; this penalty is tacked onto the monthly premium forever (for as long as you have to pay the premium, which is equal to as long as you will live).

Thus, it is impossible to overstate the extreme important of enrolling in Medicare Part B in a timely fashion. Let me say this again. Enroll in Medicare Part B **ON TIME!** Otherwise, you may be subject to a long period of time without health coverage as well as a potential monetary monthly penalty which will last you the term of your natural life.

When to Enroll in Medicare Part B If You Are About to Reach the Age of 65

If you are solely responsible for your own health insurance coverage and you will soon be eligible for Medicare, then you ought to have absolutely no difficulty whatsoever when it comes to selecting the date on which you will enroll for Medicare Part B. When you are just about to reach the age of 65, you should enroll in Medicare Part B. After doing this, the effective start date of your coverage will be the very first day of the birth month in which you reach 65 years of age.

Your enrollment period for Medicare Part B will commence three months before the birth month in which you reach 65 years of age. Thus, you should aim to start the process of your enrollment in Medicare Part B as early within this period of 90 days as is practical for you and your finances (keeping in mind that enrolling early brings with it a substantial premium every month, but enrolling late will cause your premium each month to go even higher due to the added monthly penalty and will cause a host of other problems).

Note: This an exception to the above rule concerning the effective start date of a person's coverage. If a person's actual date of birth happens to fall on the first of any month, his or her coverage under Medicare Part B (and under any other coverage associated with or related to Medicare) will take effect on the very first day of the month prior to his or her birthday month. You can try to ask what the reason for this is, but honestly, it is pretty likely that no one has any idea why this might be the case.

When to Enroll in Medicare Part B If You Are Choosing to Retire from A Group Health Care Plan after Reaching the Age of 65

If you have already reached 65 years of age and you are planning to retire from a group medical plan, you ought to schedule your medical coverage to start on the date on which your group medical plan ends. It is rather unwise to allow for a gap in your insurance coverage, and to allow a gap which lasts longer than 63 days continuously is a bit of a disaster. After you have had a gap or a lapse in your medical coverage of more than 63 continuous days, your medical history might be called into question in order to determine when or if you will be permitted to possess full coverage for each and every medical condition.

Prior to your beginning the process of enrollment in Medicare Part B, you ought to download the following form off of the internet: Form CMS - L564. Then, you should have the Human Resources department of your employer complete the portion of the form which is relevant to them. Form CMS - L564 with the relevant portion filled out by your Human Resources department will serve to verify that your coverage in the medical plan offered by your company to you due to your status as an active employee lasted until the stated termination date.

With this form which proves the date of the termination of your group health care plan and with the fact that you should have scheduled the start of your coverage under Medicare Part B to coincide with the termination of your group plan, you will not be left with any gaps or lapses in your medical coverage.

What Other Circumstances or Situations Might Possibly Affect Your Decisions Regarding Coverage under Medicare Part B?

If any of the following conditions apply to you, then your decision regarding when to begin the enrollment process for Medicare Part B may be somewhat complicated:

- Do you not have United States citizenship?
- Are you married to a person who has active employment?
- Are you possibly eligible for any Veterans Affairs coverage such as Tricare?
- Are you enrolled in COBRA or medical coverage for retirees from a group plan offered by your employer?
- Do you perhaps belong to a different category which might complicate matters?

If the answer to any of the above questions for you is yes, then you might need to seek some advice from a professional regarding precisely when or whether you ought to begin your coverage under Medicare Part B.

The professional advice you seek out ought to be from one of the following unbiased and utterly solid resources which are listed and explained in some detail below.

From Chapter 5:

If you look back, we have technically covered only the first two of these essential layers, Medicare Part A and Medicare Part B. These two parts made up Original Medicare, the Medicare system which was originally in place before a few other parts and plans were added on.

So why were the additions to Original Medicare necessary? Am I saying that successfully enrolling in Original Medicare (which consists of Medicare Part A and Medicare Part B) is not enough?

Yes, that's exactly what I am saying.

Medicare Part A and Medicare Part B do not offer enough protection in terms of health care coverage for you. Simply put, Original Medicare is not enough.

Let us see why that is the case.

The Gaps, the Flaws, and the Flat-Out Gaping Holes which Exist in Original Medicare Coverage

Medicare Parts A and B (what you have signed up for if you have followed the enrollment procedures up to this point in the book) have a number of flaws and huge gaps in terms of the coverage that they offer to you.

So what are these gaps, the gaping holes in Medicare protection coverage? These flaws, gaps, and gaping holes consist of the coinsurance, the deductibles, the copays, and the cost/expense sharing amounts that are unlimited over the remainder of your life under Medicare. These gaps, flaws, and gaping holes in the Medicare coverage seriously limit the extent of the protection which is afforded to you by the Original Medicare program (Medicare Part A plus Medicare Part B).

Cost Sharing Potentially Gone Very, Very Wrong

There is currently no statutory limit on the aforementioned flawed cost sharing components of Medicare Part A and Medicare Part B. This means that there is the potential, the risk, for you to lose an extremely large quantity of money if you are enrolled in just Medicare Part A and Medicare Part B, Original Medicare, without having purchased any additional protection or coverage from a privately held insurance company.

In fact, a calculation which someone made not too long ago determined that in the worst case scenario possible (meaning that Murphy's law applies to the uttermost and that everything which can go wrong does indeed go wrong), a Medicare patient who was relying solely upon Original Medicare for his or her health coverage, upon Medicare Part A and Medicare Part B, could be liable for more than nine hundred thousand dollars in medical bills.

What?! How could a person who actually has health insurance be charged almost a million dollars in medical expenses for his or her treatment?

Well, the answer is: because of the gaps, the flaws, and the gaping holes in the coverage afforded to a person by original

Medicare (Medicare Part A plus Medicare Part B). Those unlimited lifetime cost sharing elements can really add up.

So that is why you need other coverage beyond that which is provided by Medicare Part A and Medicare Part B. Here is where the insurance from a private company to serve as a much needed supplement to your Medicare coverage comes into play.

From Chapter 6:

In order to supplement the gaps, flaws, and gaping holes in the coverage you have under original Medicare (Medicare Part A and Medicare Part B), you should DEFINITELY purchase one of the twelve Medicare Supplement Plans (also commonly known as Medigap plans) instead of any of the Medicare Advantage Plans (Medicare Part C). This is due to the fact that all the Medicare Supplement plans offer you a complete level of freedom to choose. The Medicare supplement plans also offer you the greatest bang for your buck. The Medicare Advantage plans (Part C) are restrictive trash which eliminate the entirety of the coverage you receive under Original Medicare and which are only peddled to you so frequently due to the fact that each of these plans offer an obscenely high commission to the insurance broker or the insurance agent who manages to sell one of these trash plans to an unwitting customer. Don't be that person. Avoid the Medicare Advantage (Part C) Plans at all costs.

Instead, in order to supplement your coverage under Original Medicare (Medicare Part A and Medicare Part B), buy one of the Medicare Supplement Plans. The following four Medicare supplement plans deserve a particularly strong recommendation: Medicare Supplement Plan F, Medicare Supplement Plan G, Medicare Supplement High Deductible

Plan F (HDF), and Medicare Supplement High Deductible Plan G (HDG).

For those of you who were eligible for Medicare before the year 2020 (meaning that you reached the age of 65 in 2019 or earlier), I have already recommended to you either the super luxurious and comprehensive Plan F or the lower cost but still fairly high performance High Deductible Plan F (HDF).

For those of you who are first becoming eligible for Medicare in the year 2020 (meaning that you are reaching the age of 65 in the year 2020), neither Plan F nor the High Deductible Plan F (HDF) will be available to you, so I have already recommended to you the following two Medicare supplement plans: the most luxurious, comprehensive Medicare supplement plan which will be available to you for purchase will be Plan G, and the Medicare supplement plan which will be the most cost effective option for you will be the High Deductible Plan G (HDG), a completely brand new type of plan.

Medicare Supplement Plan F and Medicare Supplement Plan G are the most comprehensive plans available to you by law. Medicare Supplement Plan G covers everything that Medicare Supplement Plan F covers except for the deductible for Medicare Part B (which is $198 for the year 2020). These are luxurious and comprehensive plans with steeper monthly premiums, but they offer you the peace of mind that your medical expenses will be covered 100 percent of the way (aside from the $198 Medicare Part B deductible that does not get covered by Medicare Supplement Plan G).

Medicare Supplement High Deductible Plan F (HDF) and Medicare Supplement High Deductible Plan G (HDG) are a hidden secret, indeed, one of the best kept secrets in the world of all things related to Medicare and health care coverage. Medicare Supplement High Deductible Plan F (HDF) and Medicare Supplement High Deductible Plan G (HDG) offer excellent coverage at an exceedingly reasonable and low cost.

The name given to these Medicare Supplement High Deductible Plans is an utter misnomer. The high deductible for each of these plans is listed at $2,340. But a person who is insured under the Medicare Supplement High Deductible Plan F (HDF) or under the Medicare Supplement High Deductible Plan G (HDG) will NOT be required to pay the starting $2,340 of their medical bills. Instead, the person who is insured under the Medicare Supplement High Deductible Plan F (HDF) or under the Medicare Supplement High Deductible Plan G (HDG) will be required to pay only the much smaller deductibles of Medicare Part A and Medicare Part B, and if the medical treatment of the insured person continues, then Original Medicare (Medicare Part A and Medicare Part B) will kick in to pay the lion's share, the vast majority, of the insured person's medical bills.

So it is quite likely that a person insured under the Medicare Supplement High Deductible Plan F (HDF) or under the Medicare Supplement High Deductible Plan G (HDG) will be required to pay only a few hundred dollars of that $2,340 listed "high deductible." The insured person will likely pay only these few hundred dollars while saving approximately one thousand two hundred dollars a year on monthly premiums.

You do the math. The Medicare Supplement High Deductible Plan F (HDF) and the Medicare Supplement High Deductible Plan G (HDG) are clear winners in terms of a balance of medical coverage and money saving, in many situations and circumstances.

You know what? We are going to continue to belabor this point regarding the sheer awesomeness of High Deductible plans in the next chapter, Chapter 7. You won't believe how much of a misnomer the name "High Deductible Plan" is. The truth is that Medicare will actually be paying the vast majority of the medical benefits no matter which supplement plan you have in place (as long as there is indeed a Medicare supplement plan in place).

From Chapter 7:

Unless you have several horrible years in a row in which medical disaster upon medical disaster occurs to you year after year, the Medicare Supplement High Deductible Plan F (HDF) and the Medicare Supplement High Deductible Plan G (HDG) are by far the most cost effective option. In fact, in order to make the Medicare Supplement Plan F and the Medicare Supplement Plan G more cost effective than the Medicare Supplement High Deductible Plan F (HDF) and the Medicare Supplement High Deductible Plan G (HDG), your bad or worst case scenario years in terms of medical care would actually need to outnumber your good or average years in terms of your medical care.

I understand. Sometimes you just want peace of mind, and you don't want to have to worry about incurring any unexpected medical bills. If this is the case, then the luxurious and comprehensive Mercedes Benz plans, the Medicare Supplement Plan F and the Medicare Supplement Plan G, will probably be a better fit for you. You will pay a fixed amount each month as a predictable, reasonable, and fairly manageable monthly insurance premium, and you will have no surprises, since 100 percent of your medical expenses will be covered by these Mercedes Benz plans.

But if you are choosing a Medicare Supplement plan based on cost and value and you want to save as much money as possible while getting as excellent of a coverage level as you can get, then go for the Medicare Supplement High Deductible Plan F (HDF) or the Medicare Supplement High Deductible Plan G (HDG). The money you save on monthly premium costs during average to good years medically speaking (which most of your years probably will be) will go straight into your pocket.

From Chapter 8:

I would not recommend these Medicare Advantage plans (Part C) to anyone, unless you are so destitute that you cannot afford a monthly premium payment of even $50. And if you are destitute and do in fact resort to one of these Medicare Advantage plans (Part C), you will need to do your best to make sure that you rarely ever require medical attention, because if you are forced to seek medical treatment, the high out of pocket deductibles, the ridiculous copays, and the hidden fees and costly complications on just about everything will serve to make you even more destitute than you were before.

So basically, I do not recommend these Medicare Advantage plans (Part C) to anyone. As was mentioned earlier on several occasions, these Medicare Advantage plans (Part C) are just trash. Essentially worthless in pretty much every way that might matter to anyone.

Conclusion

If you have successfully completed all three of the above steps, then you now possess all four of the essential layers of protection under the Medicare system:

Medicare Part A
Medicare Part B
Medicare Supplement Plans
Prescription Drug Plans

Congratulations!